WILD TONGUE

BOOKS BY REBECCA SEIFERLE

POEMS

Wild Tongue
Bitters
The Music We Dance To
The Ripped-Out Seam

TRANSLATIONS

The Black Heralds (poems by César Vallejo)
Trilce (poems by César Vallejo)

WILD TONGUE

REBECCA SEIFERLE

COPPER CANYON PRESS

Printed in the United States of America

Cover art: Marian Roth, *Under the Water,* 1989.
Color photograph, 16 x 20 inches.

Copper Canyon Press is in residence at Fort Worden State Park in Port
Townsend, Washington, under the auspices of Centrum, a gathering place for
artists and creative thinkers from around the world, students of all ages and
backgrounds, and audiences seeking extraordinary cultural enrichment.

LIBRARY OF CONGRESS CATALOGING-IN-PUBLICATION DATA

Seiferle, Rebecca.
  Wild tongue / Rebecca Seiferle.
    p. cm.
  ISBN 978-1-55659-262-1 (pbk. : alk. paper)
  I. Title.

PS3569.E533W55 2007
811'.54—dc22

                        2007013418

98765432 FIRST PRINTING

COPPER CANYON PRESS
Post Office Box 271
Port Townsend, Washington 98368
www.coppercanyonpress.org

ACKNOWLEDGMENTS

"The Fragments of Hölderlin": *American Poetry Review*

"Ancestral Refrain," "Onward Christian Soldiers": *Big City Lit* (online)

"The Warrior for Life": *Blaze*

"Eye Center," "Before Being Numbed," "Sexual Disgust," "*Oh tell me why*": *Boulevard*

"Night Music," "*How many fires*": *Conjunctions*

"The Anecdote": *Crab Orchard Review*

"A Table Full of Wasps," "Wild Tongue," "Dogheart Dharma," "The Wound of Being," "Ghost Riders in the Sky": *Cutthroat: A Journal of the Arts*

"The Canary," "Black Water," "The First Person," "Fire in a Jar," "*the burn that the oven rack scorched into*": in English and translated into Lithuanian by Laurynas Katkus in *Poetinis Druskininku ruduo 2005 / Druskininkai Poetic Fall 2005* (Vaga, 2005)

"*Love forced to be bodiless,*" "Elephant Memory," "*White of snow or white of page is not,*" "Year of the Snake," "Not a War Song," "Dragon Hill," "Love my enemies, enemy my loves," "The Wound of Being," "Taxonomy of Angels," "Black Water," "In the Name of the Tyrant," "Night Music," "Fire in a Jar," "City bombarded with icicles": in English and also translated into Italian: *Fieralingue* (online, Italy)

"*Oh give me your hand and draw me up...*": *Homage to Vallejo,* edited by Christopher Buckley (Greenhouse Press Review, 2006)

"Fraternity," "The Butterfly Effect," "The Poem," "Black Water," "The Canary," "Editorial Advice," "The Profane, the Miraculous Hand," "*After two years you say only...*" (under the title "Tact"), "The Craft," "Disbudding," "*a* for antigone": *Masthead* (online, Australia)

"*True darkness is as rare as god,*" "Taxonomy of Angels," "The Avatar of Immanence," "*the burn that the oven rack scorched into*": *New Works Review*

"In the Name of the Tyrant," "Apache Tears," "Dragon Hill," "*Those Greek warriors*": *nthposition*; "Apache Tears" reprinted in *The Criminal's Cabinet: An NTHology of Poetry and Fiction,* edited by Val Stevenson and Todd Swift (nthposition press, 2004)

"Fire in a Jar": *Ploughshares*

"Love my enemies, enemy my loves": *Poems for Peace,* edited by Tom Hibbard (Structum Press, 2004)

"The Shearing," "Until the Cuticles Bleed," "After John Donne's 'The Dreame'," "Fiction Weaving," "*According to the myth,*" "The Too Long Married Woman," "In an Atavistic Country": *Poetry Porch* (online)

"Not a War Song": *Poets Against the War,* edited by Sam Hamill (Nation Books, 2003)

"Black Water": *Salamander*

"The Social Kiss": *Shine On, You Crazy Diamond: Poems by Teens and Their Mentors* (Sunstone Press, 2004)

"Why I Am Glad That You Call Me Wicked": *Southern Poetry Review;* reprinted in *Wild and Whirling Words,* edited by H.L. Hix (Etruscan Books, 2004)

"Ruined Pastoral": *TriQuarterly*

"First Person," "The Black Dress," "On the Island of Bones," "*The chimaera*": *Tryst*

With the author's deep gratitude and thanks to the Lannan Foundation for a 2004 Literary Fellowship, which made possible the completion of this manuscript.

CONTENTS

THE RUDDER

THE FIRE

Five comparisons of the tongue are introduced by James (3:3–11)…

1. The Bit: *When we put bits into the mouths of horses to make them obey us, we guide the rest of their bodies…*

2. The Rudder: *It is the same with ships; however large they are, and despite the fact that they are driven by fierce winds, they are directed by very small rudders on whatever course… The tongue is something like that…*

3. The Bridle: If the most unruly member of the body, the tongue, is in subjection…

4. The Fire: *See how tiny the spark is that sets a huge forest ablaze! The tongue is such a flame… The tongue defiles the entire body. Its flames encircle our course from birth, and its fire is kindled by hell. Every form of life, four-footed or winged, crawling or swimming, can be tamed, and has been tamed, by mankind; the tongue, no man can tame…*

5. The Fountain: Both sweet and bitter… one kind or the other, evil or good, poison or healing, cursing or blessing, wild berries or figs, saltwater or fresh…

"Let the woman learn in silence with all subjection." 1 Timothy 2:11

THE FOUNTAIN

Take off your clothes
Bathe in this black water
You have nothing to fear
You've done it before
The impermeable human body doesn't soak up water like
   a sponge
The sun dries the mud
The mud falls to dust
Bathe yourself
Go ahead
The earth is vast and so is your heart
which, everything taken into account,
is free of mistakes,
and was never made of mud
—Robert Desnos

"The wild is not destitute of flavor"

White on the underside
pinnate leaves
woolly stems
covered with weak
prickles

      Arcadia doesn't have smashed fawns or fish with artificial flies
embedded in their mouths, it was a Royal Coachman, I think,

Rubus idaeus
of the old world,
Rubus odoratus
of the new,

                                    my tiny gold
     hook, caught not in the rainbow trout flashing in the water's silvering
               struggle to get away, but snagged in another's
                        lure that mind
                            pulled out,

from *idaeus* to *odoratus*
in cultivations of

                    what snags and pulls free—
moving through the fallen stumps, the woods
of bent-sapling, knee-whacking, ankle-bruising deadfalls,
the prickles of primroses lashing
one's face, the glossy poisonous
leaves of the ivy, *is*
something of a dance, even

in uneven articulation, pricked to sweetness

     the berries, ah, were everywhere

tiny globes of blood,
creamy white and candle-waxed,

smooth and plump indigo
of dreaming midnight,

              and I tasted them all, all the variegations of *I adore you,*

fecund, globular, ovate,
small juicy ovules of raspberries
a bumpy roundness, grain
of flesh, pore of skin,
nipples ripened by caress
of air and sun

                        yet I could not forget that moment of good-bye:
how going home,
        I passed a crushed fawn in the ditch along the road, still alive,
bleating
      bleating up the slope where its mother had vanished, probably watching
                from the thick pines...

          and knew the uselessness of balancing
              on a sliver
           of rock, the sheer

fantasy of dreaming that was the flash
of your tender skin, among the sweetness of the berries, of tenderness that can
    only dream
of tenderness, desolate among them, downy with their instruments
of wounding, the green darkness
of their entanglements,
           hoping to be reborn, and nursed
                by their placental brightness,

          I would send you a handful
of wild raspberries but

they would fall apart in my hands
        and you would have to lick
           my fingers to taste of that sweetness

oh you couldn't, you won't…

        The narrows were impossible to balance upon, and
the rain just chilly, *oh arcadia is lost in the world and lost in one's self,*

as you are lost to me…
                  an inaudible whisper trickling
                  through the ancient realms of
                  the minerals, that
                  "bleak and mountainous district" toward the bright
                  mouths of

all that might fruit into being:

those meadows and those thickets
those blossoms and these weeds, this net of stars, that sky
so utterly black, those great frilly purple heads like sexual organs
to these wasps and butterflies, those living and vibrant nets
of shining dust, impossible to see them all, that multivariant
web of green, if our minds could ever be (we will never *be*):

                  girls nutting and berrying
                    in the raven woods

Black Water

What the blackness in the
universal trench and shovel returns me to
is the blackness in myself—earth clotted on
my tongue, mud plastered upon
my eyelids, squawking as a parrot
repeating words it cannot comprehend, an angel's stutter, a book full of
indictments of the dead who fell out of the lists of life like black water
    falling out of
my arms—how will I hang on to
my children? or cling to the table with
its pale profusions of flowers, and how
do the living ever answer the dead, their presence pouring out of
the radio and filling up the car?
                    Once every heart
had its own village, and every village
had its own cemetery, and was it enough
to undress the body one knew so well and lower it into
the blackness of the ancient ocean that broke at the edge of
the forest, at the edge of the world?... but now each of
us has put on the knowledge of God without
the power...
                Each night my tiny hours fill up with
the illiterate *x*'s and statistics of the
dead, and the ancient answers do not
answer, so I throw what *I am,* a stone to shatter the lack
of reflection, a crumb of bread to break the waters,
pushed to the lack and labor of being, where I know nothing except
I love you and that, too, arrives with its sadness, a glass of black water
held by your hand that seems so full of light.

The Social Kiss

I am so surprised that you kissed me
on the lips, I keep wondering if the gesture
was Greek, and were you open to me in feeling? For
$\qquad$ your lips tightened to
the tightest
of buds, like a child scrunching her face
for an adult gesture, so I keep thinking how hard it was to lock
$\qquad$ my own lips, to close
and clench their leisurely
span, to weld mouth, ease of tongue,
and spit, to something harmless—flat
as a shoulder, a cheek, a forehead:
a plane of skin so smooth, no passion or feeling
could hook or snag upon it.
$\qquad$ Social 'affairs'
are the purse of love, not its coinage: to be closed
while being apparently open, to never open what is so
obviously closed.

$\qquad$ Like moths to light, *no, not exactly, breeding*
(though word of grope and moan
rumor through the hallways), every gesture
can be so false, at this 'convention' of feeling, full of proposals
into words. Yet I think there must have been… something
$\qquad$ between us.
$\qquad$ (*Why did you kiss me so?*)

$\qquad$ At good-bye,
though you seem airy and almost pale with literary ambition,
$\qquad$ I'll reply in the same coin (why do I use
$\qquad$ the language of *payment?*)
and hear that silver
ringing down the sloe of your bones, pressed
against the strength of my body, my shoulder so much there,

your voice stammers and breaks as a lover's would.
Oh, all sins are sins of intent. It's not love
that makes us stutter but fear of being: to be so open
while being so closed, to close
what is so nakedly open.

Year of the Snake

All songs are sexual—
so knows the snake, smelling of the thick must

of its own self, the musk
of skin and gland, speaking

from its rock, its tree. All day, all night,
gliding back and froth,

its dry and pebbled skin
becomes a liquid impulse

that slips from branches of the willows
to inlets of earth or water.

Oh I have carried into my own house
a real bag of living snakes,

and at night I go to the darkened porch
and listen, as holding their heads motionless

above the small waves
that their movements make

sweeping back and forth
the algid and murky depths of the tank,

impelled by the agitating force
of their own unraveling,

they hiss to each other and themselves,
until I feel that lost river

of the body—its sweetness
as piercing as a sting.

Those Greek warriors

though they went home periodically to their wives
and engendered children, spent their lives
with each other lying on the frozen ground,
beneath a single blanket, on a sword's edge
with each other, until their blood poured out
and flagged one parcel of earth as theirs. As if death
were the heart's heroic kingdom, not without
convenience to the warrior state, for who
would fight with more fury than the lover
who faces with grim and terrible actuality
the beloved's death, not death by messenger
or asleep in a distant villa, but the blood
of the beloved spattering one's face,
each clotted with the other's gore? Disemboweling
makes dying sweet for those who cannot
'die' in sweeter moans, shining like Patroclus, not
in the radiant arms but the armor of Achilles,
granting Achilles a godlike fury, taking so many for
the loss of one he never murmured in his arms:
sleeping together every night and waking
every morning, men, pregnant: gravid with tanks
and machine guns, burning flags and funeral pyres.

The Warrior for Life

No, I'm not a warrior. When whatever I'm battling
vanishes or suddenly turns to me with open arms
breaking into a laugh, I feel my own weariness,
and the way the wound within me, after all these years,
is surely turning me to shadow. Battles
were different when I was a child—sword fighting
with heavy blade and cross handle, fashioned
out of wood, my friends and I astride the lawns
of summer, trading crashing blows, never stabbing
at one another but with a mighty *thwack!* trying
to shatter only the swords. Spilling our ferocious
energy, we were fountains bubbling over
into themselves, each drop of energy spent
returning quickly to us, and by day's end, our arms
and shoulders full of sweet ache, our knuckles scuffed,
we'd defeated every shadow in our bright realm:
the fenced yard and the chill definitions of our parents'
table, where girls with swords were forbidden
or disguised themselves as boys. And if the Maya
believed that only women who die in childbirth,
like warriors who die in battle, immediately
enter paradise, that's still only death's valor; so,
no, I'm not a warrior. I've only worn a warrior's face
when my son was born. His head was turned,
I had to use the pain and shudder of my own body
like a hand to guide him out, though it was the hand
and arm of the nurse reaching up into me that grasped
gently the crown of his head and turned him by millimeters
for minutes and minutes toward the light. Glad
for her gentleness, for I had to trust her, my breath
and muscles obeyed her voice as she said *wait,*
push, wait again, and all the while
her arm wedged into me was as forceful

and painful as the force contracting my body.
It was a battle she and I were fighting—myself,
both warrior and battlefield—a fierceness upon
our faces, without crying out, laboring together
until an hour later, with the pushing force of *at last!*
and a mighty groan, his head turned toward this world.
Her arm slipped out, and the baby followed:
all nine and a half pounds of him, his 23 ½ inches,
spilling out, his limbs drumming with a beautiful fury,
and as everyone did this and that—the cord clipped,
the tear in me stitched, the baby assessed and
bundled—the nurse slipped away quietly with
a pat on my arm, and I was wheeled to another
room where I lay back on the bed and put my arms
above my head and stretched out and smiled,
as if I were lying in a meadow that was only slightly
crushed, as when children roll and play upon the grass
which quickly springs back up; *there,*
on my face, that's the look of a warrior—
a happy warrior, one who has been victorious
in battling another to *life.*

True darkness is as rare as god

In Wyoming there's a monument on the coldest,
   most desolate pass between two cities,
      a pyramid

of brick with a cast head of Lincoln, penny dull,
   overlooking the streams where the brook trout
      grow stunted

by the freezing waters. At the base of the rock,
   there's a small entrance, narrow and difficult
      to enter

as crawling back into the womb. One moonless night,
   several friends and I crawled like snakes into
      the interior.

In that pitch of deepest dye, I saw how much
light ordinarily thrives in what we usually call
      "the dark,"

how even on what we think the darkest of nights, stars glow
   on the wooden ceiling, memories of color pinprick
      the dreaming flesh.

True darkness
is as rare as god: no pinfeather of light blossoming
      beneath the eyelid,

When I was five, I thought I saw God
in the sky, breaking the clouds into thresholds
   of… *a sip of its sweetness will slay me,*

When I was twenty, I thought I saw the statue of a saint
   come alive, an ocean in her eyes, breaking into
laughter… *a taste of its waters will drowse my tongue…*

Now I am fifty, all I know is this absolute dark,
some mysterious and human realm
where someone—*and set my brain on fire...*

is it me or is it you?—
lifts the other's mute hand to one's mouth,
and the hand begins to speak.

Elephant Memory

Like the twitch of my own trauma, I recognize
that elephant that, years ago,
housed in a small concrete house, a chain
around its right front leg, rocked back and forth.
Now 'freer,' wandering a field of dirt, a plaster
mountain, a drift of hay turning a small lake
to infusoria in the company of several
of its own kind, beneath a tree
with only remnants of living green…

                Not a tree of
                    utopic
      light,
      but a grey trunk spraying
                something like a scattering of
Africa,
a transplanted or residual
rain,
              the coldest current of homelessness
that falls upon us
like the memory
of our own
        posthumous

        selves. Those grey lumbering vessels full
            of the sadness of God, in the high woods
             outside Hohenwald, out of their solo
         survivals have formed a new herd. A female
tribe like hyenas or bats, the elephants cluster around
           the one that they've made their new mother
and greet each other with trumpet and twining trunk.

        Not a high tree in the
           orphic

ear,
but a forest of
improbable
pachyderm,
dense
body of what
survives.

> To us, they decline touching or being touched.
> Not because like *noli me tangere,* they desire to ascend
> to some more than bodily realm, but because
> they remember and brim over as we do…

> watching them from our human distance—
> so two-legged and alone.

…*still* is rocking back
and forth—no chain upon its leg.

Not a War Song

Why should I, searching the thesaurus
for synonyms for *chant* and *cadence,*
try to make various and alive the unremitting
noise of war? Army cadence, battle chant,
if the behavior's unique to our species,
each bird or whale or wolf in solitary
call (though I'm not sure that I believe
this when all the wolves my neighbor owns
start howling to a police siren), the words of war
are as dull as the armor of the ruthless
Diomedes who stalked the goddess of love
to harry and harass her from what had been the fields
and green pastures of Troy, now decimated
to an excremental slab of mud and limbs.
He pierced her veil of stars and fog to slash
her hand where bone meets palm. So war
is dependent for its reason and its myth
upon the desire of wounding someone's
lovely form, and the poet must be a solitary
singer (not necessarily nightingale, perhaps
common wren or western meadowlark,
its voice tightening across the distance),
singing a bleak and awkward beauty against
the commonality of war.

Ghost Riders in the Sky

You can no longer say where the photo was taken;
it resembles so many Western landscapes: the sun
going down in the fire of its own glory, the ship
sailing off in flames. Yet you know the figure
that is lost, that is always lost, is your brother,
his purposeful saunter of one lamed
like any failed god or hero, fate's mediocre
toe lost to a bicycle chain, his heel caught
in his mother's grip, who bent over and scooped
up his wounded foot in her apron. Yet still who managed
to stride, to stroll, in the too-large hand-me-down
boots on his feet, though the toes curled up, and
all the kids laughed at his Rumpelstiltskin-curly-toes.
He would not take the boots off, but clamped them
on, striding into the playground, already caught
in the haze of the golden dream of being, beyond
ridicule, beyond pain, beyond any hope of rescue.
He kept on striding away, though his spine was bent
and his vertebrae shattered, though he ached from the fury
of unnamed horses and uprooted posts flying
through the air and nailing him in the back, from punches
thrown in parking lots, from barbed wire unrolling
its private range in scars along his arms;
he always got up and strolled away, as he did
the last day he put down his chaps
and his lariat, hung his leather skin and left
his life hanging neatly like an abandoned flag upon the railings,
as one who went armed, who went forth, who faced
himself at the edge of the water and fell beneath his own hand,
and even in death, his eyes have that look, honed
beyond any horizon, trying to pierce that godforsaken golden haze.

The Poem

No, it's not cold, not an artifact, but
a living, breathing word, which moves to you
as I cannot, which makes you blush a little
and makes me nervous at your response. Or
if is cold, perhaps it is the cold necessity
that makes one carry one's own heart carefully
like milk poured into a saucer, the shallowness
the social world allows—yet even the care
and the tactile sense, that bowl balanced
upon the tips of one's own fingers, seems
to belong to the art of the body's moving.
For the feelings themselves are not altered
by being written upon a page. As if untouched
by speech or language, though it speaks
again and again, that chaos keeps trembling
within ourselves, all the more clamorous
for being awake, as a flock of birds might burst
airward at a human sound then settle back down
into their thicket, but with a clutch of song,
broken warbles and those just beginning, so
when I said in a poem that I missed your kisses—
not of lips but of being, an *x* upon a page,
a signature, the beginning of a word
for which one will have to search forever
in any dictionary, all that's left when
our tongues are broken by any kind of fever—
who's to say which is more real? This ordinary self
who clacking down its keyboard of errands
would only dream of such a thing, or this other
who crosses the threshold of being, as easily

as a drop of tear or blood or the sweetness
derived from plants fluxes across the permeable
membrane between one cell and another, as if
all this world were one body, as if from any
beginning, every you and I were one.

The Anecdote

Even then I knew what she held out to me
was an erotic spark in the damp wood
of my sadness, so I don't want to diminish her
gesture, to make her into a literary anecdote
on that coldest of days, with the air smelling
like a fire that has just been extinguished,
and a breeze so cold from the depths of the ocean
that everyone who stood about on that hill
overlooking the sea shivered and folded
their arms over their chests, as if to keep
the chill out. It was one of those aimless
gatherings, and she and I had found ourselves
telling the secret histories of archived
griefs, when someone appeared with a pan
of steamed clams. I know now they were
of the genus of Venus clams, *Veneridae,*
a species without teeth and with rough lips,
named for she who rose from the sea, probably
because of that moist bud in the relaxed clasp
of the shell, those shells lying side by side,
the hinge of flesh sprung open, sprung apart,
and that some poets say it's an exhausted
metaphor that compares cunnilingus to eating
clams, but all I saw that day was so much death,
so many shells clattering at the bottom of the pan.
I tried them reluctantly, surprised by their salty
tidbits, the smoky flavor of their pearls of flesh,
but even so, it wasn't until much later that I guessed
what she meant when she came up to me afterward
and offered that red raspberry, *polpastrelli,* holding
it out to me on the tip of her finger. "Try this.
Eating raspberries after eating clams. It's very sexy."
By the time I understood, I would see her leaving

with her husband, and she would stare at me
over such a distance, such a dark and living depth,
that she stumbled a moment and missed the curb, taking
just one step toward me, leaving that moment—
which *is* a gift, this story I'm telling you—even now
still poised at the tip of her finger like a nipple,
ripe, erect, at the tip of my tongue.

A Table Full of Wasps

Outside the tables are full of wasps, so fervent
with buzz and saccharine drip, while, inside,
I could be drowning in the depths of
the ancient mine, that poisoned water table,
instead of sitting at this table of words, bitter
and blue, where the eyes of the girlfriend of my host
are so mysterious with exhaustion, I search
for some sign of *her,* some flicker or
bright fin of vanished being,
as this afternoon, in this odd restaurant,
I looked down into a mining shaft around which
the tables were arranged, and was surprised
by the shine of two common goldfish
and a huge white carp motionless
in that lead murk. But nothing in her
rises up to meet me; she is cooler than
the waste water at the bottom of the shaft,
leaking upward, as it does, from some wound
in the earth. Why is such a lovely woman
tethered to such a man who, grizzled and wheeled
with mislaid intentions, snickers after his own comments
with a breathless *ehehehe*? She stammers
when I ask her what she does—What do *I* do?—
as if it's years since she was asked, then drags out
the sheepish boredom of her nine-to-five,
even though it's clear to me, it's her labor
that lets them both live in their tiny desert
house as she goes on to lament the secretarial
position that makes her too exhausted
for her painting—her art an afterthought
to his life. I think perhaps she loves him, she says
he reads poetry to her each morning, soft with wit
and insinuation, but, as the evening wears on,

I see the flat faces they turn to each other,
as if masking what's no longer there, the gaze
of a long marriage, not quite the same
as the deliberately cool and measured neutrality
she wears when looking at the man at the next table
or the net of the smile she casts toward me.
In the days to come, I will notice so many other
young women attached to some ex-hippie,
a potbellied, disheveled, middle-aged Dionysius,
still believing that love is free, greying locks
hanging around his shoulders or in a ponytail
knotted at the back of his neck, an aging god
of intoxicants, spouting in public he's male and female
when making love to his wife. Over and over
I will see some she incline her head
in that cute gesture with which a child tries
to curry favor, or as a horse, caught by a bag
of sweet oats, will hold its head still,
its muzzle stealing sideways to lip at the grain
while being fit with bit and bridle.
So over this table and its sweet mouthfuls,
it's her *thought* that she holds captive.

"Love my enemies, enemy my loves"

Oh, we fear our enemy's mind, the shape
in his thought that resembles the cripple
in our own, for it's not just his fear
we fear, but his love and his paradise.

We fear he will deprive us of our peace
of mind, and, fearing this, are thus deprived,
so we must go to war, to be free of this
terror, this unremitting fear, that he might

he might, he *might*. Oh it's hard to say
what he *might* do or feel or think.
Except all that we cannot bear of
feeling or thinking—so his might

must be met with might of armor
and of intent—informed by all the hunker
down within the bunker of ourselves.
How does he love? and eat? and drink?

He must be all strategy or some sick lie.
How can reason unlock such a door,
for we bar it too with friends and lovers,
in waking hours, on ordinary days?

Finding the other so senseless and unknown,
we go to war to feel free of the fear
of our own minds, and so come
to ruin in our hearts of ordinary days.

Ancestral Refrain

Just now, I hate the sound of the bagpipes. Each morning
as we go from lecture hall to classroom, dozens
of children, bussed-in to practice for a week,
march up and down, pumping their arms and elbows
like flightless birds trying to take flight, changing
their individual breaths into a chorus of keening,
wild dirges, the piercing of Scottish war songs.
Yet, the woman who turns to me this morning
is rapturous at being Scot. "It's so serene, that lilting
refrain, it reminds me of my heritage," her face tilts
like that white island catching the breaking sun.
"It's 'Garryowen,'" I choke out, "the damned song
Custer played before each 'battle.'" Such *élan*
swinging into the waking hours, the bayonets
flashing along the banks of the Little Washita,
to finish off the children hiding in the brush, to fashion
cartridge pouches out of the vaginas of women, and last,
to slaughter all the horses, for the army first tried
to cut their throats, but the animals were too afraid
of the smell of the white men, so the cavalry called
for more ammunition—it took 800 rounds to kill all
the horses—and Custer's final tally listed 103 fighting
men killed. *In truth, only 11 could be so classified...*
the other 92 were women, children, and old men.
We're both startled by my vehemence; her Scottish
fingers twitch in her tartan scarf, as if trying to unravel
that loose thread of undisclosed genealogy, and still
she pleads, "I didn't know, it sounds so sweet"; "oh,
it's the voice of my ancestors." And, of course, she's right,
it *is* the voice of our ancestors—all those war cries; in any language,
the children rehearsing, trying to get just right,
each note in a song of slaughter.

Sexual Disgust

The kiss of the leech
in the irrigation ditches of childhood,

blood-colored with mud and debris,
was a mouth full of delicate sleep,

so none of us could feel the pencil-thin bodies
attaching to shin or ankle

to fill up like glossy balloons swelling
with that blood that, in them and us, we found

disgusting. Since then, considering the human modes
of attachment—the furtive grip of that poet

trying to steal the magic of a curl of hair
on a distant shoulder—and why even Christ

cried out when that woman who could not stop
bleeding merely fingered the hem of his robe—

I think the mystery and splendor of God
must also tender us in the mouth of a leech.

Circular orifice, full of tiny teeth and all the nightmares
of *vagina dentata,* so that soldiers in the jungles

were said to fear nothing more. What disease
of the heart makes us move so quickly

through these waters, thinking this proliferation—
all the forms of love and regeneration—is just the muck and murk

of being? Shuddering in sunlight, we scrape our skin
with knives and cast our repulsion into the waters,

filling it with the filth of names and our own severed
genitalia. All the while, all the while

the leech lights up the depths with an ebony sun, full
of the mystery of shared life.

Make your own garden,

                    peach
                            apricot,
scarlet,
          rust bronze to primrose,
softly scented inflorescence,

a very gentle mouth
of dragon,
every color but blue,

                    Antirrhinum majus
magi in the yard, their quirky
flowers are endearing, even in the casting hour of the ice rune

as a child, did you ever discover how to press
the sides of the flower tube
between your fingers
to open the dragon's mouth
and snap it shut again?

Penstemon palmeri, wild, hardly larger than a fat muffin,

                    Don't be afraid to try it!

the pollen melting its buttery
yellow on all the backs of the bees,

and modern cultivars—
         penstem-flowered,
                  open-throated types,
                            bicolored, bisexual,
10–15 flower spikes of tubular
flowers

velveted, rounded
upper and lower lips.   Tiny mouths

of bestial color.
3–4 cm, zygomorphous,
one plane of symmetry,

        anti   *rhin*
        "like"   "a nouse or snout,"

commonly
called in Asia a "rabbit's lips,"

        in Oriental astrology, shy and given to melancholy,
        very creative and inclined to withdraw into its burrow, the rabbit
        in some calendars is not a rabbit, but a cat

in Holland "a lion's lips,"

        all that petal, furling hair of dark color, the way the mouth
        opens so wide, thick lipped and the anthers resemble
        teeth

in the British Isles: toad's mouth, calves' snouts, dog's mouth,

        O scarlet burgundy of dragon lips,

                I am planting you outside

with your vulvar mouth so velvet
colored, so rounded lipped, green ovary, royal
bump, white buttery dew of anthers
like antlers, stigma, filaments, style, sepal, and
gland hairs on the anther like strands
of silver tears,

        before you die in my house

    no honey bee can enter in, tight-lipped
to protect the pollen, cannot open up the mouth
called by some botanists
"the power-consuming mouth of
the flower."

        Oh, we all know what they're afraid of,

that softness, those tiny
teeth hinged upon
its upper surface,

       another
mouth that gives utterance
to flesh, a third eye
that dreams
in sweet dark earth, flowers, flowers, flowers, flowers to:

    Drink me in the morning

while the bumble bees
buzz and brumble in,
sucking from the bottom of the tube, carrying
away a drift of pollen, powdered on their thoraxes,

          The body sounding all its throats

in the shade of garnets
that ear all beauty, stolen

from the fire festival, which is what some call the "hour of snapdragons,"
when raisins and sweetmeats are lipped
up, snapdragoned from glasses of burning brandy.

        Oh, the wind
is full of nothing
         but these desires
    so gracious and so fascinating, nosing
        gently the fence
they lean upon, the borders they are owned by,
      dispersing scent and color
    in the air, copious self-sowers,

spreading stem and bracts,
so sensitive to the influences of gravity—

constelling every shade but blue,
disarming deceit, breaking all
charms, digging with a teaspoon,

I am filling the desert with softly scented animal mouths!

Dragon Hill

To love is not only to gaze at the other, but
to gaze *through* the other,
so wherever love sends me, I look.
                             Among the painted
locust, the blue-footed booby, the lava lizard
whose skin still burns with the earth's interior
fire,
            Buddha returns, as a land iguana,
                          wearing the same mysterious smile,
to sit in a small cave hollowed out of lava,
his skin like living rock.
                    In the Galápagos,
isolation has made infinite variety
            out of one monotonous cry. A laboratory
in evolution, we call it, the defunct eye of the tuna
against the bottom of the boat.

Here the earth is not your body but the heaven you think
            you could be—the shimmering patina
of the lightfoot crab, the happy angles
of the frigate birds shadowing your furrowed head,
           and Buddha in a lizard's visage, wearing
the spiked crown.
                  Human, animal, or divine,
there's a large blackness in the center
of the iguana's forehead,
                murky as a galaxy
coalescing, a new face forming, and in the depths of the new
cells, a third eye, its eyelid closed, dreaming

the heart's refrain: *Out of so much,*
so little; out of so little, so much.

Wild Tongue

We're not all lesbians at this bar and grill (not yet?
not practicing? only in heart?), *chiaroscuro* as the room is
    with expensive ambiance and dear cuts of meat
and fish overlaid with nouveau fruit sauce, it's clear
    that the most manly woman among us, older,
      wearing cowboy boots and a turquoise bolo,
    is probably neither entirely straight nor wholly
queer. When she begins to confess her 'secret'—
      it's her holding of a piece of land, acres
    of sweet desert; its muddy roads, its remote
sublime have four-wheeled deep into her being.
She's probably someone's heavenly grandmother,
      as I'm still someone's heavenly wife, despite
    the separation. *Appearance does not really appear,*
but it appears to appear, yet, for a moment, it seems
      our conversation may open up unexpectedly
    or shatter into awkwardness over the word
        girlfriends: how in the rainy summers
of our youths, we all played with our girlfriends,
    (what do I mean by *'girlfriend?'* what do you
mean by yours?) It's only then, as one of the younger
    women (the most lovely, so silver with bracelets
    and earrings and a noticeable ring) laughs
that I begin to guess her inclination, *Does it really*
    appear to appear, or only apparently appear

to appear? It's a long way from Plato's symposium
to this bar and grill in Arizona. At that ancient feast—
whenever a number of individuals have a common name,
they have also a common 'idea' or 'form'—only
men reclined upon the couches, and only the love
of man for man was love's ideal, the impulse
toward some boyish form becoming the ascension
of being to some ever truer realm, as the souls
of men became pregnant and gave birth to
"not only beauty, truth, and goodness," but
"the heavenly bed, created by God... a heavenly man,
a heavenly dog, a heavenly cat, and so on through
a whole Noah's ark," but no heavenly woman, much less
a heavenly lesbian, for since Aristotle, "Lesbian rule"
has meant that measure made of lead so it could be bent
to a curved or crooked wall. Because we are all women,
how can we speak of love? In the beginning, banished
from the realm of discourse, assigned to love's servitude
not its speech, to be love's body not its tongue,
so no one here speaks of her feeling, much less thinks
to make it another's measure. In our mouths, the tongue's
a knife, each word a wild edge, where we stammer
only our own wound, a drop of blood sensual
on the tongue, a distinctive taste of salt, more
mollusk perhaps—wrapped around an *I* of sand—
than pearl, a syllable of milk or nipple, some
private body within the body, the *you* behind
your eyes, as if being itself were poetry—passionate
with nascent and protean neologism, full of the gaps
of being, the oblique richness of a depth in which we
begin to glimpse each other, mysterious and solo
as we are, black stubborn pearls of being.
If we spoke of Plato, and we don't; each of us
was banished from the womb by virtue

of having a womb, to this unpredictable realm
where each of us would have to discover
her self, that wild tongue—never delineated,
even in shadow, upon the philosopher's cave wall.

THE BIT

Oh give me your hand and draw me up
from the suffering of this mysterious realm.

It's hard not to be anthropomorphic when
the Great God of the Hamsters doesn't hear
the insistent shriek of the newly born hamster
that has been forgotten by its mother
who carried off the other two. For all its febrile
struggling into life, like a red thread trying
to knot itself to her absent flesh, its not yet
open eyes are already buried in the natal nest,
while its mother runs back and forth, torn
as she is between the newly born and her other
litter—just three weeks old, the size of thumbs
and still trying to nurse—she's equally frantic
to nurse and wean, while the male hamster
sniffs after her, already driven to mate again.
I know that life's a relentless process, uses
us up, just to make more mouths squealing
in the famined twilight. Yet when my son
who's eight years old and cares so much
for each particular hamster that he knows
the number of golden hairs upon each tiny spine
and the exact wrinkle of each nose asks me to pray
for his hamster family, I say I will and do, wondering
in which direction to turn my face, to cast my voice
into which darkness? For we ourselves
are all there is—our remedies, to buy another cage
and separate the older litter and the father,
so that the mother is restored to calm. *O measure*
of our strength, and limits of our helplessness:
there is no other god of mercy than us upon this earth.

a for antigone

Oh mother… she moves as if toward someone, catches herself and stands
   there mutely
Where is he?

What? How long have they been looking? Have you all been sitting here
   like this the entire time?

You mean none of you went to look for him?

*who has, who has been searching the fields and the edges of the marshes for
   hours, with sirens and with dogs, who has been combing the thickets
   and dredging the muck of the entangled cattails…*

You are sitting here then because you know he is dead. What difference
   does that make?

*he went out riding on a horse, no one knew where he was going, or why he
   went riding in that direction, he was on the wrong horse, he was on a
   horse named Messenger, he had his weapons and his shield and his
   armor and he went riding past the small and squalid yards and the
   ramshackle houses and crossed the intersections and stopped for nothing*

What difference does death make to the heart's affections?

*some stranger cutting the weeds in his field and stacking them into a bonfire
   to be burned saw him go riding by and was so struck by the strange
   sight of a man arrayed in armor riding by that he looked up from the
   smoke with his eyes stinging—how acrid those weeds are in the burn-
   ing, how a flame touched to them catches in the wind and races into a
   hot conflagration*

You entrusted his fate to strangers

*everyone is burning their fields, but only one man noticed him, and said that
   the man who rode by seemed to be scanning the horizon, as if expecting*

to see something there, as if trying to see some landmark, some sign for
the direction in which he was going

and his body to dogs,

a messenger of some disaster

or are you waiting for him to come home? thinking that if you sit here
long enough, that you will dream him walking back into the door,
with that crooked grin, mischievous at riding home, in the direc-
tion where he thought home was

he was headed into the snow, but the man who was burning his fields said he
was riding, purposefully, like someone who knows where he is going, a
strange sight, a man in all that gear riding a horse as if going to war

What does it matter that he was on the wrong horse, that he rode away
on the wrong horse?

one's always riding into death on the wrong horse

confused like our father that day I ran into him by accident in the hospi-
tal, I was waiting with someone else for someone else, and there he
was, my father, his face the color of lint, asking a stranger which
way should he go? I went up to him, he kept saying, he had to get
back to where he was *in the beginning*

He must not have known, the other man said, when he rode over that hill
that the hill was the roof of my house, I designed it myself, I built it
myself, a house buried in the side of a hill with a roof made of earth
and grass, I wouldn't have guessed that a horse's hoof would go through
the roof, plunging through the layers of sod into the interior of my
house

What do you mean?

so strange, the other man said, to be sitting in your living room and hear the
noise and the crumbling of the ceiling and look up and see a horse's leg,
up to the knee, that trimmed but unshod hoof flailing from the ceiling

You thought we were all happy?

*war in this house, war in our blood, war in our heads, in the neural net and
the nerve endings, in the brain's grey dream, that terrible root of dis-
cord and division, it all begins here in the seed of the sperm, in the eye
of the ovum, in that terrible war of mother and father, the children
divided like spoils among them*

Oh, yes, I remember, mother, when he was little, he was playing with our
sister in the grass under the clothesline, and you pointed them out
as the very image of peace, the very image of happiness,

how bright they are, their heads the color of sunlight, how peaceful

(what you meant was not like me, how bright they were, how dark I was)

playing quietly

Oh, I know, you didn't mean it. You've never meant *anything.*

*it was all war by stealth, by quiet, by evasion, by the obedient smile, for they
were plotting among the grasses, distributing the wealth and gain of
the game as ruthlessly as any tyrant and perhaps more so, colluding,
just the two of them, just the few of them, smiling, in the enchanted
circle of exclusion, no one there to break the lie, no troublemaker to
scream out, to make the war-disguised-as-peace apparent*

As an admonition to me, always that reproach for being the dark one,
the one dragging your gaze back to this dark, all those fissures in it,
where he's missing now

*as long as the lie was unbroken, the shredded papers and flesh hidden in the
grass*

Yes, I remember, you said the hail could kill him, if it hit him on the
temple or the soft spot of his head, he would die, so I was running
and running, trying to keep him from the hail, you thought it was
funny, my panic when the tiny wagon got stuck on the curb, and I

wasn't big enough to lift it over, I thought you had said I would
kill him, but you had given me the weight of his life

*the storm ignored upon the horizon, the hail falling out of the sky, into all
the soft spots of one's being, someone else's weight*

Yes, I know you didn't mean it. You never do. I'm sorry to remind
you of it.

*waiting and waiting in one room, a group of mourners for the arrival of the
corpse*

How could you think we were all always so happy?

*into the fields of course, wherever he is, follow the thread of the body, the
thread of my grief, my mouth that used to call him "little brudder"
will call out to him in my breath, without words, and his corpse, with-
out words, will answer*

I don't care if it is a rule,

*a proper hour for hello and good-bye, that particular moment when the
slaughtered and baked bird must be brought to the table, when we all
must arrive and sit down in our usual places, a banquet of death, spit-
ting out always the bones and the flavor,*

I seem strange to you? Does any of this seem *not* strange?

*who has, who made up this rule, no one, everyone, the phantoms of the mind
issue out of some commingling of the many in desire and in fear and
clench flesh in their iron hands, until the body is wound up in barbed
wire, the tongue bridled, and even the mind cannot move, but like
shackled feet, cannot move more than an inch to left or right*

Well, I'm sorry to disturb the banquet of his death

*he had to die, didn't he? for if he hadn't, what lived in him might have killed
us all, probably at some great banquet, several pheasants that he had
killed sitting on the table in all their golden crackling flesh, while you*

sat there, smiling, so glad at the gathering of us all at one table, so happy, being all so happy

that's the last thing, he said to me, you know, that we should all get together, on some great occasion, and have a new beginning

this is it

oh don't look at me like that, you always have that naked face, like a plucked bird, all raw pale skin and the stubs where the feathers were

the new beginning that he imagined,

what law, whose law, without speaking, without a word, can come up with a rule, it's like a phantom that emanates from just sitting together, some marsh fire or swamp gas emanating from the rotting weeds, the fallen stalks of the cattails decomposing into the thick sludge, how is it that you all know it without speaking, and I who am faulted for speaking can never know it?

unspoken, yes, such laws are always unspoken

Oh, he knew those laws, he has probably died out of obedience to them.

don't let my family see me like this

No, I don't think he was riding away, he was riding toward, how happy he was

had bruised all the soft spots in him, so he went out riding toward something else:

No, I'm not trying to make you feel bad.

all my life does seem like the gloss the living paint on the face of the dead

Yes, I know I say terrible things

wasn't he already three days dead, wasn't he lying on the grass looking up at the sun and seeing it as an omen, wasn't he shouting at strangers in the street, wasn't he muttering to himself as he sat in the yard and pulled the grass up with his fingers, wasn't he always at war, wasn't he the only casualty he ever slew

No, I don't want to make you feel bad.

every family must have one terrible child, the one who says all the things that the others will not say, being so attached as they are to that happiness in which they think to bathe and drench themselves, as if the only happiness possible is the happiness that is blind,

Yes, we were happy, we were always happy, I'm going to look for him, I'll say whatever you want, just let me go, since the lie of whatever I must tell you is forgiven in the truth of my going

in your twilight with your ghost of the rule enlivening the room, sit here with your emptiness of being in the fullness of bodily grief, neither cry nor cry out, make these minor adjustments of the curtains, sweep the dust from the fields that he brought in on his boots out of your house, discuss in endless detail the crooked wall that he built and how the stones that he meant to place in order never met your specifications, say angrily how you never took his shit, how you refused to put up with it, how you told him so on many occasions, how you made him speechless with your certainties until he could neither cry nor cry out and all that warred within him became a mute haze of unpredictable acts, riding into the distance

What? No, I don't want some more tea.

I should never have let you interrupt those quarrels I was always having with him, for the sake of peace, for the sake of happiness, so that instead we could have the peace and quiet you wanted, full of the minutiae of our latest task, the endless law of shopping and dinners, I should never have let you silence the war between him and me, it was the truth of the war within us, the war between us, and it was the only embrace we had left to give each other, struggling in the grip of words, for the truth of our own lost feeling

No, I'm not arguing, I'm just going,

what rule, what law can keep me from the corpse of my brother, what love can turn away from a beloved face,

Yes, you can stay here, they'll bring his corpse out to you sooner or later

though kissed by flies

~

Muttering to herself

the edge of the water, to the edge of the water and lie down in the grasses, in that circle like the shape of a wheel crushed into the grass

he could have been me

I could have been him

a swamp that looked just like this one, more cattails, a sea of them in the black muck, so thick that it would suck the boots off one's feet, not as much thicket,

what? yes, I can…

sometimes the only thing left to the living is to identify the dead

why did he go down that other road? is it ever the other road? where was he going? he probably thought he was riding into more life, riding *home*, a common mistake

yes, everyone else is back at the house

but no one is truly there, it's a house full of ghosts, the ghosts of this body lying here, this body alone is real

the injury to the horse, the animal in oneself, all that blood guilt, it was that terrible moment of recognition when we realized who our parents were and what they were to each other and what that made us, misbegotten, zygotes of the impossible, only four of us, no one else, no other relative, no friend, no family, a house of four

children, that terrible dream of happiness casting its spell upon the
seed of the sperm and the eye of the ovum

why can't I touch him?

to say my brother, my brother

what crime is his body evidence of? it's so hard to know where it began,
      its tendrils reaching and intertwining through our nerve endings,
      into the grey corrugations of our brains, the rule of the fathers, the
      law of war, its rootlets and saplings reaching into the thick black
      murk of the human skull

no I don't think anyone murdered him

it's hard to say who, there are so many, it goes so far back, there were those
      who showed him when he was a child images and practices of war
      until he trembled and cried his way out of girlishness, there was the
      father who spit him out of himself, in his body and then in his words,
      there was his mother who gave birth to him out of the abandoned bit-
      terness of herself, there was that ring of boys, so golden and laughing in
      the light, who circled him and pummeled him until he became harder
      than any fist, there were all the fists in the fields and in the streets and
      in someone's house, there was one woman, there is always only one
      woman,

how long are you going to let him lie there like this?

his hand is still reaching toward his punctured chest where the blood has
      already clotted but it is as if the hand still remembered and were still
      trying to comfort him for what it had done

yes, he had been troubled for a long time

they said he seemed to be getting better, someone said he seemed happy
      yesterday

no, no one wanted to kill him,

he was the only one who wished he was dead

~

Once I climbed into an open grave, I used to walk through the cemetery
talking to myself, in a cloud of feelings and words, because I
thought the dead could hear me as the living could not, and one
day I came upon an open grave, its sides so sheered from the cold,
the severed roots of nearby trees like white knots of muscle in it,
that it looked as if the earth in the shape of a coffin had been cut
out in one gesture and lifted out, leaving this rectangular descent,
though I could see this was not so, because the earth was heaped
up in mounds beside the grave, at a respectful distance, and I won-
dered what the view from death was like, so I jumped in. And I
could see nothing but the sheered sides, it was winter, the ground
was frozen and my fingers pressed against it left no impression, it
was a sleek flank of impenetrable substance, and chilling to the
touch, there was nowhere to look but up, into the sky, except the
sky was sheered too, without horizon, without the intricate laceries
of the trees, the interruptions of the buildings, that so frame the
sky and give its expanse that sense of depth and endlessness, as eyes
may, being framed by a face, give us that sense of unplumbed
depths, of an infinitude of light gazed into or gazing back, so the
sky was flat, a rectangular shape of blue, without depth or horizon,
the eye could not swim in it or dream, it was like the eye of a god,
impenetrable and without variation, just a blue rectangle, and I
knew even the heavens are cut in the shape of a coffin, but I
couldn't bear that gaze very long, I became impatient, and wanted
to get out, but I realized that I did not know how to get out of the
depth into which I had descended, the walls were so frozen that
they allowed for no grip or purchase of toe or finger, my hands
slipped from their sides as they have fallen away from the chill cold
of someone's expressions, as a child reaching to someone's leg may
feel such a resistance in the flesh, that her hands slide away, I was
sliding away from the earth, into the earth, into its coldness, and I
became afraid, panicked almost, that I would not be able to get
out, what would the mourners think when they came to bury the
corpse that was meant for this grave and found another, strange

48

and uninvited, lying within it? Only the place where a shovel had slipped and made a gouge allowed me to slip one toe into it and then I scrambled out, only the wound allows one to escape, its howl propels the body back into the air, as a child howls out of the womb, no punishment beyond being born, beyond what it sees and knows.

Eye Center

Among the nearsighted, the farsighted, the afraid
of going blind, and those who like myself with perfect vision
are surely losing it as they grow old—Milton blind to his daughters,
my dear sweet Ruth Stone sighted to every loss—I am trying to find
    some way
to send contact lenses to my daughter on the other side
of the continent, while lumpy Betty tries to smile
as she whacks the computer monitor "up alongside the head,"
and Jane, pale with laxatives, raises her hands, flopping
both backward on her wrists, like a seal's flippers
to show how useless she is, while Mr. B., the glittering
head clerk, pivots back in his silver sideburns
and pontificates about some distant HPO to some
question that has forgotten ever being asked, The Doctor
Himself strides through the office, and it's clear
from his new laser-corrected stare and the tightening
at his temples, and his own suddenly windswept mane—that poseur,
Shelley, for instance, if he'd lived to be fifty—that Zeus
is the God he thinks he is, serene, Olympian, luxurious
in clouds, stopping only momentarily to rain
a bemused grin upon his minions. The phone rings
for the eighteenth time since I began my vigil,
and, this time, it's Sherry, back from lunch,
whose face is painted on so thickly, it looks
like an odd Western version of a Kabuki mask,
who answers it and says to Mr. B., "It's for you.
It's someone named Alma. She wants to speak
to you." Faster than he can process a check, Mr. B. snaps
"Tell her I'm not here," and Betty and Sherry and Jane
and I all glance at one another, while Sherry hesitates,
perhaps wondering how to lie
to a strange woman on behalf of a man she doesn't like.
Mr. B. turns to my order, all business now. *Alma*

hangs on the line, and, if it is truly his soul calling,
Sherry's not lying when she coolly mouthpieces
into the plastic: "He's not here. He just stepped out."

The Canary

So difficult to hear beyond the provisional racket
of the self, the small whisper of being,

yet sometimes I think, in the waking dream
after meditating, that I can feel the deepest pulse of all those I love,

slipping into a distant kitchen for a cup of water
or tripping down the morning stairs into the noise

of a different city, so far away, in whatever hour it is
wherever they are, that the pale flash of an elbow

is so tangible and of such sweetness that it falls
as lightly as a hand placed on that acupressure point

that hurts above the heart. I don't know if it's
bodily memory falling as imperceptibly as

the gold pollen of the juniper tree, or the dream
of the cells of my body imagining

the world into flesh, some centerlessness
of being, but it's as piercing as the cry of the canary,

not the cultivated roller that sings with closed lips
in a cavernous cage while the waiters

in their white uniforms and hats marked "Mother's"
yell out orders and the names of customers—

the special of the day, a bowl full of trash, a cup
full of mud—until one hunches one's shoulders

and pitches into mourning, but the original
nondescript green and yellow finch,

discovered in 1475 on the "Isle of Dogs," which sang
only when it was alone, a song so piercing

because it had to travel across
all the distances of its world.

Dogheart Dharma

Oh love is stupid but it's true, all day I feel
as if I were a dog on a chain—you know, the way
they lie there, bored in their beings, as if their bodies
were loose skins full of emptiness, too alive
to truly fall asleep, too dead to be fully awake,
and, then, periodically, for no apparent reason,
they'll jump up in some biting fit, snapping
at their own limbs, teeth closing on the fine
hairs of their own coat. *Oh my desire*
keeps me pacing a circle of dust. I thought
I had broken free of the chain of existence, but
now I am born to a pack of lives—each one
trembling with happiness at hearing my name
called by your sweet voice, your mastering gaze.

Fraternity

"Oh brother!" I say when you remind me
of that fight at work. Years ago, you were smelling
the bouquet on someone's desk, their blooms surprising
in the crushing scale and noise of the power
plant, its pulverized coal covering everything, black dust
filling the fine lines in any ungloved hand, and you were homing
in on their color and scent when Jones came up behind
you and said, "Why don't you smell this fucking
flower!" and when you turned, he pushed you back,
his hands flattening against your chest, his greater
size and weight crushing you into the desk, until
you moved in all those ancient and practiced moves
of striking snake and flashing heron, and pinned him,
harmless, cursing, to the veneer. Later you told the boss
you wanted a meeting, and he said "Okay, on Monday,
we'll get that Indian," as if suddenly your equally swart
skin were allied with his, but by Monday
Jones was already in jail for assaulting his family
over the weekend, and you too had gone home in a fury
over the subtleties of those flora. You could never say
to him what it meant to stand there opening
to the garden of yourself as the petals always open
toward the interior that is always sexual, always erotic,
so that Jones, moved by the woman in himself, toward
you or toward the flowers, had to harden to fist and curse,
for you too were a stone, sharpening your knives.
How else extinguish the woman who lives within a man...
or the man who lives with a woman? For by saying
"Oh brother!" I too have turned the word of fraternity
into something of a curse. A soft exclamation of woe
in which I can glimpse for a moment my brother
lying in an ancient swamp, dead by his own hand.

"Onward Christian Soldiers"

Once there was a little boy who marched
around his mother's kitchen in cloth diapers
and a red cowboy hat singing the refrain,
"Onward Christian soldiers, marching off
to war!" All the words he knew until he grew
into the rest of the melody, learning the second,
third, and fourth verses, singing it all the way
through, every night, until forty, until even his wife
knew the song by heart. So that hearing the words,
full of rust and creaking armor, blasting out
of the mortician's sound system, I smile
for a moment, seeing again that little boy—
his plump legs, his round belly, a sweetpea
chanting cheerfully around the kitchen, as if
he had not marched off to war—that middle-aged man
in a coffin made of cardboard for burning—himself,
the only casualty of that battle, himself,
the only foe he ever slew.

The Butterfly Effect

to Joy Harjo

When the newscaster feels sorry for the short life
of the butterfly, the biologist says sternly that
"The butterfly is only the caterpillar's means
to reproduce." In his view, the worm in its verdant
leaf is the origin and end of being. But from
the backseat of this cab, where we both have lapsed
into silence, careering down the concrete
canyons of San Francisco, so many attractions for the "I"
in the rush of people and traffic, it's the butterfly
my eyes follow—that yellow swallowtail,
which floats and turns above the asphalt, its brightness
like a gesture, oblique and random, which unfolds
itself and continually surprises as it falls
and skims the air with a gesture complex
with accident and desire. The updraft
of exhaust sends it spiraling. Over and over,
it seems it will die on some windshield or radiator
grille, and when a bus comes around the corner,
it seems certain to be caught up and perish in the wake
of that greater body, for death has its own gravitational
force, and what can this fluttering do against the pull
of such a force field? *Fluttering hand, your hand*
is as cold as a wave of water, fluttering heart, I think;
ever since my brother died, something has been loosed
within me. Like a hook that doesn't quite fit its eye
or the hinge in my hotel room on that expensive-looking cabinet
that slips down, a quarter inch off-center, only when
someone opens it. But perhaps it's no more than
the butterfly, that bright scrap of being, in the thermal drift,
the current that bears it upward and slightly to the right
is the current that saves, so that it hangs a moment,

imperishable in the air, as the bus lumbers past into
a slot along the curb. "I thought that butterfly was going to die,"
you say as the cab driver hits the accelerator and guns
our car around a corner, and I'm startled into "me, too,"
both of us laughing aloud with recognition, finding ourselves
with the same eye—amid all the wealth of the modern city—
following with anxiety and desire and so much longing
the path of the butterfly.

Ruined Pastoral

At first the amber
seeping out
of the ancient
fireplace tearing free
from the foundation
seemed only a mystery,
a river of gold light
that you could plunge
your finger into
and taste, but then
you noticed
the cobwebbed
filth of mice,
their tiny droppings—
how ancient
the hive was
and how dangerous
in that desert
where lungs could fill
with the waters of
hantavirus—
the sound of nothing
filling the house,
invisible bees and
death in the sweetness—
your finger to
your tongue.

The Too Long Married Woman

So, it came to this, she could barely bear
to be touched, though she was glad for that
moment in the kitchen, tense with containers,
scrapings of delicacies adhering, floating
in the sink, and the other woman who turned and walked toward
her, holding out her arms, extended
from her shoulders, those most human wings,
to gather her up into her *she* happy birthday wish whispering
into her hair and neck, and so went home,
momentarily buoyant, for it was not the body
she couldn't bear: for she could rest against
the edge of bone beneath the white collar,
the finer weave of skin warming against her,
almost impersonally, as a child falling into
a field rests against the curve of density
of grass. No, it was the fingers of mind or feeling
touching her most private body, the eye
bedazzled by the blue dance, the imagination's
bacchanal, all those invisible weddings of eye
and word, the tactfulness of some word reaching
into the private pleasures of her bath, the scent
of crushed and collected herbs perfuming
her soul's pillow, the sensitive not prying
into her sadness, rain kissing all the leaves
in the mind's invisible bed, all the feeling so
felt in another until she felt herself, so open
as if she had no skin or membrane. Then how to keep
herself from all the criticism of how she held
a wine glass or did not hear—*oh right away,*
or spoke *wrongly*—the noses sniffling in protest
from her cigarettes, the broom and finger pointing
out the cobwebs in every corner that she'd
forgotten to sweep away? Falling upon no skin,

stung as if by wasps beyond all nerve endings,
how to tell the criticism meant to rescue one's real
self from that meant to destroy, having no sense
of self at all? So she went in and out of the house, retrieving
winter's snowy wood, splitting stumps with a hatchet
to red aromatic heartwood, kindling one fire after
another, then washed each time the smudge
of ash and smoke from her hands until her skin
chapped, breaking open, as if dismembering the self,
she would know herself by wound.

Apache Tears

In the rock bins of my childhood, every tourist stop
sold Apache tears—obsidian drops, smooth and velvety
in the hand, obdurate, until, held up to the light,
each became a smoky being, a cloud pregnant
with rain in that desert—making a story of the beauty
of grief out of a tribe of Apache (really no more than
an extended family) who were trapped at the edge
of the cliff (by the Mexicans some said, others
the U.S. cavalry), who all leapt to their deaths
rather than being taken captive, and the tears
they shed before dying turned to wild stones
at the base of the cliff. I don't know how many
tears I bought and lost; a galaxy of black stars
in those bins, and yet each time, I looked through
that landslide of sorrow, thinking if I found
the right one and held it up to the light,
I could see entirely through it. If it's ever possible
to see *through* human suffering: beyond knowing
in any climate and any time, there are those who are turned to stone.

The Wound of Being

So still and quiet in the depth of the wood, so intent
upon the shred of white birch bark that I am trying to
write upon, to fashion into something like living paper,
that the green depths around me, unwatched, become
alive, the bushes trembling with the lives of the squirrels
and occasional birds, the throat of the frog once again
opening into song in the water, the step of the deer
moving toward the sweetgrass, so in my not being
here—my attention, that restless thief, that peddler,
paused as if suspended above the blades of the grass,
the blue succulent leaves of the skunk cabbage,
their lovely globular heads—I hear the pulse of the earth,
its many breaths, how it goes on without me…
the drift and rustle of words moving in the depths

behind my eyes, the advent of true feeling. As if attention
were meant to be nailed to a shoe or a pencil in order
for the deep presences and the deep absences of the self
to begin breathing. Once, for days, I became an absence
among a nest of wild kittens, a large saucer of milk
on the floor; each day moving the bowl a little closer,
I waited and waited, almost unbreathing, until
my hand flew out of its own accord (at random,
it wasn't toward the one I'd thought I wanted). Seized,
black and starving, the kitten shrieked and turned
to stitch me with its needle teeth. I carried it home
in both hands, clinging to its feral body as it clung
to me, its eye tooth anchored in my index finger, so present
and piercing, that I felt my self in the bloodred drops

as a welling up and falling away.

Taxonomy of Angels

No, I do not think that angels love. Not as
    lovers do, or as a mother who sweeps
  her child into her wings, for why would they
    stand about and debate the hell or heaven
      of that chilled soul that drowned itself
      in a bitter lake? Mere messengers they are,
  who but obey. Or mirrors of that faceless gaze,
which we are meant to take on faith, pitch umbilicus
    to our most distant father in the sky, though
  they themselves are full of nothing but light. Flaring
      out their wings, they appear before us
      and we begin to burn, hoping in our ashes
    for something other, *brighter*, than we were.

Perhaps, they were never more
        than God's fireflies,
                lightning bugs of the divine, abdomens
flashing the unspeakable
        names of God,

for, regardless of whether they are waving a sword
        over the dragon or the sleeping infants of the Egyptians
        or holding aloft the flower
of the annunciation or sitting down in the acacia shade
        to eat the milk and honey that an aged couple has just
        stooped to serve them,
           or casting living fire
upon Gomorrah,

        there is something cold and insectile
about them, something proto-evolutionary,
      that makes us tremble,

so that we love to see them, flickering up and down in
the dead of night,
            and yet don't want to touch them, to feel the scales
of their wings, the scrambling of their tiny appendages

            upon our flesh or caught
in our hair, so segmented, so cold and certain in their grip
            to reproduce and propagate the light. That light born
                        of a chill that withdrew
so far from the earth at the beginning, that ever since
            we have been trying to draw it back, to warm
                        it back to angel flesh,

painting its messengers as mothers, soft feminine faces,
            leading children across a bridge, a guardian
                        glory at our elbows, a ministry
                                    of solace to guide us back
into ourselves. But they were never
the human given wings, but another kind
            of being, inscrutable as
                        lightning bugs,
                                    their flesh flaring in a message
                                                that was never meant for us.

                        So caught up
                        in the flickering

                  that time embeds within each cell,
                        to divide and multiply,

            that, while they fly and mate, they do not eat;
                  they starve and feast on passion's sting

            and fall to earth only in the bottlegreen moments
                  between one mating and another, their legs

                        attached to a brick wall
                        like tiny hands losing their grip.

So palsied are they, quaked
by what they want and want and need...

Yet, detached
from the meadows and fields,

rising up out of the soil
where, for months,

they have been worms like us—
pale groping things

of appetite and fear—
when they rise, they seem

the very wings of desirelessness.
They light up and are not burned,

but drift like lanterns on a tenebrious sea that no wave
but time can make go out.

So the eye
flies

to them
as to love.

Before Being Numbed

What was most disturbing
wasn't just the squished face
of X and the bruised brow of Y, or
the sounds that came from both their misshapen
mouths like the cries of the humpback
whale, or the way Y flopped her hands
together like two deformed rabbits
huddling under one branch, while X slid
to the floor like a bag of rocks,
that disturbed the dental office and all of us
waiting there and aching with memories of root canals,
but their 'caretakers.' It was hard to say
which caretaker's fist had bruised
the eyebrow of Y, or if the bruises were just
the 'accidents' of neglect, letting X or Y
routinely fall to the floor—for X, with her head
that looked like it had been pressed too hard
between the palms of God, did, just then, spill
out of her chair and clip her eye on an armrest.
One of the caretakers dragged her up by the wrist,
like someone carrying a dead chicken by its feet,
touching as little as possible while still dragging
her away. And in the cubicle of my own appointment
and pain, I could hear X or Y singing in
childish cadences, the lilting unintelligibility
that could have seemed like the undisguised cry
of the animal heart, naked of intervening mask
and mind, except that they sang together
as only human beings can, while the caretakers joked loudly
about what it would take to knock X or Y out,
how one of them would wake to a pillow
full of blood and never know
it was her own. "She eats like a pig even

with her broken teeth," and it wasn't clear
which one the caretakers meant: X in the dental chair
or Y on the floor or all of us strapped into our chairs
for the grinding of our teeth.

The Profane, the Miraculous Hand

I keep telling myself I should be happy, my house
is full of roses, the full-throated scent
of the yellow ones on the counter, the bright
sunrise over the table, and even, in front
of the house, every plant blooming as if
it had been brushed by the rain of the miraculous
hand, and even the unusual chill of the wind
at night seems to make the roses thrive,
and I think, I think that I am
loved, but my feet each morning
are deep in the throw dark of water,
I can hardly move with remembering,
and when I lie down, I see that rabbit
frozen in that ancient field ringed by dogs, caught in the open
past the cattails of the swamp, surprised
on that most lovely of mornings, its body
already full of the dark cold current
of the underworld.

                    In the darkest dark, I thought
                of you as if I were listening to the pulse

            of being and was thought back to life by thinking
                that my ear rested quietly against your chest,

                as my infant ear once rested
        on my grandmother's breast, as my child's ear pressed

            against the earth, as my ear that longed for death
                    listened to the snow,

                    some part of me, all hearing
                    listening to the words

you say, but more importantly, to
what you are,

so I drifted back into this room
where the fire in the candle of the miraculous hand

had burned all the way down to the wrist,
so that fingertips and the palm with its cunt-like wound

were illuminated
by the brightness of what I felt for you,

and knew—born in a month of snow, out of the blackest
waters of what is stillborn,

that burns hell in a child's heel, and brands
a being with the birthmark of an angel—

the divine is
whatever calls us into being.

That Domestic Animal

My damn cat brings me a dead songbird,
wren or finch, I don't know what it is—
I mistook at first its folded grey
for a strangely shaped piece of lint
in the cubicle beneath my desk—nor which
cat for I have two: Cricket with her dense
body and stubby legs who jumps down
from every shelf so reverberatingly, I call
her the Black Bomb, or Ingrid, the quiet
Russian Blue, whom I call Gritty because
her coat is stealthy with dust. They're always
leaving me offerings—the mouse upon
the threshold when I return from some
trip, the redheaded grosbeak on the sill—
but death is different in the front yard
or even on the threshold, than Death
on a particular morning, crawling *into* the house,
carrying a warm form frozen in its warm mouth,
tongue and tooth salivating a fluff of warble and whistle
into a smoothly folded, iced, silenced thing, Death
triumphant, *affectionate!* as if anyone would be happy
feeding upon dead songs torn from the air.

Wearing the Horns

Ill, I am ill, though it began innocently enough, sweetly almost with the
erotic imagery of horns, something spoken to you, the tiny buds of baby
goats erupting, so soft, and hard beneath all that fine hair, still smelling
of milk, I shouldn't have mentioned it, for it reminded me of disbudding
the goats, how I would burn out the horns, why do I use that word,
dis/bud, to remove the bud of something, those tiny horns beginning to
erupt from the skull, just knobs of velvety skin and an underlying hard-
ness, how could I have been so brutal, it's not that it—the disbudding—
was brutal, but that I was, in the terrible stench of burning hair and skin,
I used this iron, a round copper tube that had a handle, and I'd heat it in
a propane torch until it became red and glowing, and then I would hold
the animal while I pressed the iron to the bud and rotated it around it a
few times, burning through the hair and skin, leaving a dark brown,
black stain, that slick feeling of the metal sliding around the bone of the
skull making a ring of dead skin, dead veins, dead nerves, so that the
horn would not grow, or that terrible feeling of the skin sliding away,
while I felt in my own burnt hand, I had been driving from Phoenix to
Flagstaff, up that short abrupt ascent from nearly sea-level desert to mile-
high forest, and the car overheated, and as my sister and I stood there,
with the hood up, wondering what to do, at some point, I put my hand
on the radiator cap to check it, I knew it was a mistake the moment I
touched it and my skin began to melt, the radiator cap was a quarter-
turn open, steam was beginning to hiss out of it, I realized it would erupt
into my sister's face—her beauty, her eyes—still peering down into the
engine as if into a well and that it would scald her face away as it had
already taken the palm of my hand, so I tried to shut the cap but my
skin just slid across the cap, it was already detached from me, I couldn't
turn anything, my hand was like a stripped screw that can't be turned
into wood or tightened, and so I put my left hand on top of my right
and used the weight of it to anchor down my own skin so that I could
turn the cap and I did, and managed to shut it, but I've never forgotten
that feeling of my own skin slipping away, and all the while the kid is

fervently struggling and crying, I would be holding it in my arms, I would be burning its horns, for while there was always another to help me, I did everything at one time or another, I took turns, sharing these terrible tasks, the tattooing of the ears with green ink and the way the needles on the punch would go through the flaps and bleed like pincushions, the way I would do it all at once, unable to bear more than one morning of the stench of burning hair, the way they would open their pink mouths, their tongues like frantic things trying to climb out, stabbing the air, so I'd tattoo the ears with the identifying numbers and then disbud the horns, and oh the shock of it upon them, a web of shivering throughout their bodies when I let them go, sometimes one kid would stagger, as if stunned, back to their mothers and the milk bottles I held out to them, and I thought I had good reasons for this, for their horns grew and they would get stuck in feeders and break their necks or they would impale each other when butting each other aside or they would impale us, though I don't remember a farm on which this actually happened, except I do think there was one guy who had a buck die after it snapped its neck in a feeder, but perhaps that was apocryphal, a myth, one of those ancient stories that persuade us that I must do the worst before the worst happens, and what could have been worse than what I was doing when I was disbudding the goats, nothing worse, except when I killed some of them, always the male kids because there were always too many, and so I'd kill and butcher them, one or two usually, glad that there were just one or two, and so one of us would hold the kid and the other would hit it on the skull with a hammer, in that exact spot, in order to kill an animal you must draw an x from eye to opposite ear and hit the center of the x, and so I brought the hammer down upon the intersection, the skull collapsing, for they were so young so slight of skull and bone, everything in the world was of a greater hardness than they were, as metals are rated and numbered for their hardness, so in the metallurgy of existence, they were the softest of things, the domes of their skulls only a little harder than the specific gravity of eggs or flowers, and they would fall upon their knees, as if flying through concrete, a strange trembling would overtake them, and I could not cry or tremble because the worst thing, then, in that strange realm, seemed to be the idea of

faltering, of hesitating, of not hitting the center of that *x*, which would cause a dull thud and require hitting the animal again, and so one (I) (you) tried to make one's arm the falling of a sword, the sword of that angel that blocks the way back into paradise, irrevocable, so I would bring my arm down and the hammer down upon that invisible *x* that my eye drew upon each sweet head, and then as the animal convulsed and lapsed into unconsciousness, I would cut its throat, and the blood would flow out, there never seemed to be that much of it, and even that seemed "better," better than the way the other farmers did it, which was to just cut their throats and let them hang there bleeding and dying and strange sounds coming out of the cavity where the voice of the cry had once sounded, and it's just a word on the page now, *disbudding*, I haven't done this for years, I don't know what I was thinking, and sometimes one of the children was in the house, and I would tell her not to look, not to listen, because I did not want her to see what I thought I had to do, and yet she always knew so then she would look and listen and even if she did not look or listen there would be that pastoral day driving through the mountains, the loveliness of the meadows, and somewhere by a corral and a running stream, I would say to her, oh look at the sheep, how beautiful they are, and she would look, but just then I had already real- ized that the men on the other side of the corral were butchering the lambs, that one was struggling in the man's arms, that one was already hanging, its throat cut, and she would see this and turn away from the view and the glowing of the meadows and the mountains into the space wherever it is that one looks away from death and it would be too late for me to say anything, what could I say, she who I called lamb, she who now carries a small toy lamb with her wherever she goes, though she is grown now, and what could I say, and she would feel in some way that it was herself hanging there, and how can I speak of this to you, how can I bear how brutal I was, how can I let my hand live, when I thought it was love that brought me here, to this meadow, where it began innocently enough, sweetly almost, with the erotic imagery of something spoken to you, the tiny buds of the meadow evoking, merely evoking,
heartflesh soulflesh eroticfleshbud you

We should have turned back

on our way into the Marine Fest, at the skeleton
of a child whale making a gate with its bones.
Its skull, like white stone, carved to
vanished eyes and tongue reminded me of that ancient
bard who said poetry began in "the sound
of wind over the sinews of a beached whale's skeleton,"
silent now, devoid of meaning, its vertebrae lined up
to serve some architecture of science and frivolity,
the fins, minus cartilage and muscle more clearly
delineating the ancient feet that crawled away
from dry land to vanish into water. But it was only a toddler
among leviathans, the same age as my youngest
who pulled me past the skeletal warning
into the T-shirt painting workshop in a rainbow tent.
Inside, a flock of children held up white fluttering
shirts, now stenciled with the shapes of fish
upon a coral reef; the hue of voice and color
was so distracting, it took too long to realize
the children were painting their T-shirts
with the freezer-frozen corpses of fish, dunking
a school of them into vats of paint, then slapping
with the sound of lifeless hands falling upon
a morgue table. *Oh clapping is the sound
of death.* We fled, driven out by the strange
melody, as if in the heavenly choir, amid the lilting
hands and strings, someone had blurted out, *instructively,*
"in the beginning... harp strings were made of a drowned girl's hair."

He was falling down a precipice,

                                    he was
entering a dense thicket, he had
no refuge, no friends, no allies,
the sun of his life had set, he was
terrified, he was running
from the messengers of the Lords
of Death, he was embarking
on a great battle

                          but *his heart was*
already pierced, he had fainted
on the streets, he had stared at the sun
with his eyes wide open, he had lain
upon the threshold of strangers, he was
filled with the Wrath of the Lord,
                                 drunk

with rebuke,
        he drinks from
the cup of trembling in a swamp
of stagnant waters where his flesh and blood
are turning back to earth,
                      in the shade
of a cottonwood, shimmering
in the waters and the sky, reflected
in the double mirror of this world and the next,

he sees himself as a wrathful deity,

his face has been taken apart and hammered
back together, *he is a broken hinge,* his eyes
are a shattered door,
            his mother *appears*
carrying his corpse in her teeth and rattling

his bones in a cup, he *is given over*
to his enemies,

                        they pursue him
through the street, they tell him to "bow down"
so they might pass over,

                       and he lies upon the ground
and makes his skeleton into a bridge
that he *now passes over* into the next world,

O mother of god, O faces of mercy, tell me
this is not my own brother, lying here
at the edge of the water,

                       the flies kissing
his open mouth, his hand stained with his own blood,

let some numinous presence have kindness upon him, carry him away,
for all I can bear away is his body, *and here*
there is no escape

The Craft

Sad twin of the river
and sea,

caught in a drift
of current,

I will sail
and sail

past the gaze of
Rimbaud's cold black pond

where a boy and a boat
drown in a French farmyard,

or Vallejo's caravels,
freighted with sweets,

floating in a stock pond
in Peru. Slipping past

my sailboat
of sibling rivalry, racing

my brother's
across the pale blue pools,

and finally free
of my father's tiny galleon

coffined with dead frogs,
a swamp of dead warriors

setting sail
into the Anglo-Saxon funeral

of the setting sun.
I will be only myself then, or

the child that I was, a girl
giving to the river

the boat that I carved with a knife,
its scrap of dead tree,

its mast made of a branch,
its sail, a pierced

and resplendent leaf
of autumn.

At the end,
the heart is only a

leaf-wording,
leave-taking,

that launches its homemade,
handmade boat.

Why I Am Glad That You Call Me Wicked

When Simone Weil said it would be wrong
to think the mystics borrow the language of love
for it is theirs by right, though she didn't call it
the heavenly song of cock and cunt, perhaps that's
the inevitable conclusion of the sacred heart wounded
into a womb, an arrow in the hand of an angel
piercing such a depth in the body until it's beyond
what the body knows, delirious among the lilies
or tasting the sweet meats of that table. Yet
whoever the mystic woman is, she's not 'about'
sex; it's not some sexual fantasy that she lies with
in the dark mansion of God, sleeping every night
in a different room, curling herself to the different shapes
of emptiness. It's not some narrative of first
he this, then she that, that makes her tremble,
being naked and open to nothing but that
noche oscura, when with love inflamed,
the saint runs out of the house into the hills,
for she remains, asleep and dreaming, and in God's
innumerable rooms, innumerable forms and shapes
of love, she lies down with them all in the depths
of her body and blood, until every vision and icon
shines with a glimpse of the forgotten and atavistic
feminine body, pouring out of her as if out of the nipple
of that blue stone embedded in the miraculous
hand, as she herself becomes her own threshold;
no faces remembered or imagined flicker across the hymen
of her mind, for it's not a penis, even God's, that she imagines,
but the form of herself, the *knowing* of the body
of her own feeling, as in the Old Testament it was said
that Jacob knew Rachel or Lot knew his own daughters,
the knowing of the body allowed only to men;

women, only the known or unknown, as she is known and un-
known but as she knows herself as she knows the other
that she is not: she enters herself, with fingers
of melting wax, of cold cucumber, with a thumb
of glow, with all the abandoned utensils
of domestic life, with a stalk from the forsaken
garden, and with the lost wing feather of the angel
of death and with the voice of a baby's cry
nursing on the vestigial milk of the mother of mercy.

Beyond Ithaca

What I meant was in the face of such cruelty,
all that one can say is love. "Poetry
begins where death is robbed of the last word."
But when I wrote, I saw that "except love" might
be read as a gesture of farewell; then I had to
explain, and explanation is the death of poetry,
so you became confused and thought I was saying
good-bye. *How could I?* Up to my ankles
in that trench that was filling with blood to call up
the ghosts of the dead for directions to the underworld,
I knew, if I knew anything, that I loved you, among
all the others that I loved, their bodies filling with light.

Night Music

I

"voice" is not only a manner of utterance

  there is so much light in the dark water

but a *mater* of being,

  the waterbird seems to be fishing for nothing

so that form, even the apparent absence of

  but light, its beak, a thin needle of splendor

form

  threading the waters

is the attempt to create

  all the dark at its back, luminous,

another order

  like that river which was believed to circle

of time

  the ancient world where we are still

that river which is full of prehistories and intoxicating

  watching for the winged messengers

drinks offered to lips of water

  so that we always begin with the simplest of faiths

naked or the color of blue berries

full of the dust of ourselves

2

that word, like many words,

I kept confusing

has a *person*

the vessel of the supposed

buried within it

hero with the monster he went to kill

so the mask is fashioned

its eyes as many as mercy, its mouths as many as death

until we forget ourselves

trying to stay alive as a happy animal

though at moments in another's eyes

for what is a love but that

we still glimpse the face of the beautiful daughter

night music

peering out beneath that white skull

of the human heart

a strange and terrible prize

3

there was this ancient rule

    full of a pain

that words could not be

    as I am now

uttered

    my own horned toad

as a thumb jammed into the mouth

    weeping tears of blood

would choke off crying,

    out in the garden,

piercing the ear of that most distant angel

    the fear of love, the fear of death, the fear of not

who falls to the ground like a dead wren

that idle cat brought home

4

he said that everything would change

    I was listening to the radio

if the word *radio* were used in a poem

    dancing not in body but in mind

because what is a poet

when suddenly I am, oh, somewhere else

but a night music

in another realm of being,

so full of pain and sounding so much like you

and in that world, too, I love you and love you

for what are 'you' finally

and I'm holding out my hand to you

but the very body of night,

your hand resting lightly on my palm

a folded wing,

our fingertips just touching

a tree full of birds

as we begin to move…

A music

> **So close and reserved**

It will not show itself

> **Except by a dark light**

5

where am I

I've gone miles past the turn back

when I'm absent-

to my life, to the errands of the hungry

minded?

cats and dogs, which I do easily, mindlessly

my mind, humming,

loaded down

with bags and papers,

walking into the house

my skin still strange and full of that night music

into the bright and busy rooms

THE RUDDER

The First Person

Who is this *I* who loves you, never having
glimpsed you in any clearing of the fog,
who returns to me full of words
and feeling, drawn up from a mysterious realm?
Who arrives with a wounded hand, a scar full
of flowers, a body filling up with black water, and falls
into the white skin of the birch—that white skin
of my childhood that I was always trying to carve
into paper, to write upon with words. Is it
even "me" at all? For what does it have to do
with the sweltering room that the tiny fan tries
to keep cool or with the dogs that howl
at all hours, or with the fury of the neighbors
slamming their doors? Yet it seems more truly
me; how will I follow, who will I be, now
that I'm no more than a shadow? How can I
turn away from what it tells me: this *I*
who believes it can cross any distance or hear
the whispers of god flying along the farthest
trajectories of everything that's lost, who fingers
the pulse of those who have died, who finds
its face in a well of dark water, and who loves
you and loves you as if all the beauty of the world
has lain down in your arms.

Fire in a Jar

Some plucked from flight by sweep of net
or grasp of hand, immediately eclipse
and flicker out. A drift of stars becomes
mere green beetles scraping the glass bottom
of a jar. Other kinds go on flashing, ardent
no matter how captive they are, lighting
up even the smallest heaven. And still
others make a haze of their own longing,
dispersing themselves into a diffuse craze,
becoming a drop of sexual sunlight falling
upon the transparent world. Glass eye,
glass heart, glass jar, in which we try and keep
our flickering selves, all the light in us is sexual,
a luminous persistence—a heaven or a hell.

Revision: Medusa's Gaze

Two women in a boy's room
                    to see pet lizards
            must bend
                            to child-view,
                so I lie upon my elbow
                            to fit my eye to:
the size of little fingers,
color of dry leaves, living dust,
fluid rivulets of quick flesh,
                    flitting
among the rocks and artificial plants—
                        the hands of the gecko
soft moist
stars
            pressed to the glass—
and she kneels beside me,
                    the excitement of boys and lizards,
the anole leaping to the topped screen,
            and becomes some other age, 12–18
                                all the ages in between,
                    telling the story
of her rose-colored
python,
            whom she so loved she wore her living in her hair,
its sleek roseates
            coiled lazily around her neck or entwined
                    within her auburn hair,
so still and close,
that other
pulse, beating
against her throat. The snake,
                        she says,
would greet her, arching its face

up to her nose
        and kissing tip with tongue.
She meant to tell in the beginning
        how it frightened
others,
when the snake
        adjusting slightly its warm embrace
or shifting its grip
        at the vibrations of some word
        beginning
in her larynx, would startle others'
somnambulant glaze of greeting to wakefulness
        of snakes
uncoiling along their own spines, with that snake
coiled in her hair, though
she, too, was altered
        in the seeing, made strange
when another shrieked, involuntarily, in body quivering backward.
Which also made the snake
        nervous
        sometimes tightening
around her breath.
But the story gets away from her
        as the anole leaps out of our sons' hands
and suddenly
        we're somewhere else,
        some other age,
so lovely
and so lively-locked,
        that flickering tongue kissing the tip of her nose,
        I am a Serpent, I am Love,
        I have been an Adder of the Mountain,
        I have been a Serpent in the River
all mythologies become all mixed up:
        the *Nathair*
        of entwined adders

the *Naddred,* Druidic name of *bards,*
       or paradise of the Medusa, so lovely and so lively-locked,
before trauma made of her a horror,
most chilling gaze of flesh of victim
          banished to peripheral shores,
the egg, the shed skin the swift and silent penetration of earth.
                 Emerging from her self
      singing some other song, so long forgotten,
            forsake the ability to wound for the power to heal,
          what she gives me is a dream
whispered
over some
      dish that left a fire on our tongues—

miraculum,

a living girl with snake
so loving in her hair,
         that, when she leaves, called back
      by the oven's timer, we're floating
in some lyric cloud, so fluid and fluent with shape-shifting
      we shed our skins upon the floor,
and could never wish to leave that realm where waves
                 break in
         upon the *I,*
         oh, with
a laughing
blue. When my son and I say good-bye
        to her, she's disguised
again
amid a drift of plates, the orange flesh of a yam
       steaming open beneath the knife
         she holds in her hand,
          her own dinner,
everyone else already bending to the savor upon the individual plate,
       I'm not surprised

she follows me out into the rain,
her arms opening to late winter night
    so delighted
        at the lingering feel of rain
           and chill upon her skin,
the air transpires out of all wounding,
        some other age, or any age, so gazing at me,
I cannot look away,
that blue
    of eye breaking to
infinite of love and healing,
and in her hair,
    that radiant snake,
        invisible but coiled,
so that I want to embrace her or say *I love you,*
for seeing her as one with snake
        still living in her hair, transformed by gaze
to love
not fear, to fluent
shifting possibility
not frozen mirror,
        but instead say
          oh go back in,
it's cold out here,
    she laughs and does not move to go,
        as if she heard what I have not said,
so standing there, so looking back.

Oh tell me why

do we fear passion more than we fear war?
Why those ancient warriors outside Troy
feared Aphrodite more than devastation, why is she
the only god driven, shrieking and wounded,
from the field? Why is it better to die
by one's own hand than to enter the depths
and be changed? What would have happened
if my brother had entered the water?
I remember how when he was a boy
he'd throw himself from the high tower into the blue
eye of the swimming pool, over and over again,
laughing as he leapt into the eye of his fear,
so why was he so afraid of entering
the water? Did he fear all those things
that had dried up in him to dust, would rise up again
with a thousand hands and shapes of water, to fill
his cowboy boots, to drown him with desire,
until he would have perhaps felt his body
filling up like a sponge with longing,
his heart filling with light? It was the desert
he had become, his leathery skin, his hooded
eyes that drove him to the water, where that shallow pond,
a remnant of a vanished river, an atavistic spring,
would turn him green again, and everything
would have to change. He'd have to wash away
his loveless marriage and his crooked wall,
he might have run away with that golden girl
he kept painting, he would have gone looking
for her, rolled up his sleeves and exposed
his chalk pale arms to sunlight, shed the snakeskin
boots, that uniform of the cowboy, those Levi's, that hat
sweated to the shape of his body: he might have *become* her.

The Avatar of Immanence

for Gray

In the narrow straits of sea to the North,
in a narrow boat that channeled north,

a woman cried for a lost son,
not her own, but another woman's.

Her cry pierced the slate grey waters,
and her voice fell like a pebble tumbling into the depths.

She was mourning, too, in a quieter way:
herself, her own son now grown beyond her,

able to navigate and captain himself
through the shoals and barriers of that distant grief

(for it was his friend who had died), the news that arrived to her
only in his telling, so far away, by secondhand.

All her cries were soliloquy,
as she moved through those isolate waters, caught

in the nets of the self, on a deck
in the middle of nowhere, still propelled

by the tasks of ordinary life—
to pick up the fish, deliver the freight,

the chores of money, the cost and the price,
the boat going north, and her heart

like something caught
for butchering, tethered alongside.

When out of the depths,
a killer whale, its black-and-white calf nuzzling beside it,

drew starboard and kept pace
with the boat. As she wept, the whale rose to the surface

with its mysterious eye
and looked at the woman.

For thirty minutes, the whale swam with the boat,
cow and calf swam with her grief,

and she was comforted by the gaze
of that tiny eye, such a small *self* in a fluid mountain

of bodily presence, love like a depth
of black and white sounding a sea of grey.

There were others, later,
who scoffed at the story,

believing whales incapable of empathy,
the natural world devoid

of mercy, or convinced only by accident
or coincidence, that perhaps

the whale mistook her vessel
for another whale, a strange metallic messenger

of its own lost pod. And even the most
sensitive of poets would doubt

that any whale would tune its fine sonar
to the sound of human grief.

But she would tell and tell
the story,

on countless occasions
overlooking the sea,

her dark wave of memory
surging through halls of the halting stammer

and the crippled poem, or at mercantile
gatherings, anywhere

really, retelling the story, trying
to get it right, to tell it again

to one soul among many.
For she *chose* those to whom she told it,

as the whale had chosen her,
that act—*a breaching*—

of sympathetic correspondence,
between herself and that arctic world.

And, sometimes, one soul adrift
listening to her voice—

her eyes closed to the moment, drifting
back to the lap of the water, the interruption

of her cries, the rock of the boat,
the fog erasing the horizon—

would see for a moment the grey world looking back
in the living gaze of the whale.

In the Vocative

"Dear friend," or "dear beloved," why not—
"dear dog," "dear cat," or perhaps,
considering the rareness of the feeling,
"dear aardvark," or "dear endangered
species"? Though at the risk of sounding
as if I'm giving the I'll-never-be-your-
household-pet-speech, unlike that translator
who's variously a blond Chihuahua in a froth
of heels or a French bulldog in relation
to the original text, I have to say each term
so brings its food bowl and its collar,
its water dish, and even its allotment of lawn
and sidewalk, that something in me begins to howl
itself (myself!), back to the very *aleph*
of inarticulate claw and feeling, in that soul's wood
where language falls, when it does not fail,
as light falling through the leaves, and where in the *omega,*
all that matters is that you call me.

"Don't cast your pearls before swine."

But what the Bible doesn't say of the dispersal
of pearls is that the whole world can't be swine
nor the self just a scattering. After all this is
the book where the favored son is the one
who's dwelt among pigs and there's that other
parable of the pearl of great price, which you
always find in someone else's field, and having
found, must sell everything you own to purchase
(so difficult to reconcile with the commandment
against coveting). So I'm arguing back
from what's implied; for in any living language,
love swarms in the silent depths, the gaps,
the absences, what is not said, so I'm arguing back
from the words of the warning addressed
to the swinish world to the silent blessing
of my bowing to you. There must be some
moment of being and time when we are meant to
bow to one another, out of a deep reverence
for one another, a love beyond burning, to cast
our pearls before one another or whatever
we call the equivalent of pearls, since they're just
metaphoric for the riches of being, whatever
we've hauled up from the cold dark depths
where we are so alone, or perhaps it's the cold
dark depth itself that we offer to one another,
when something like the god we thought
we didn't believe in begins to shine in our eyes.

The chimaera

to begin with, are all beautiful, their sleek flanks
of hurricane, their personification of cloud,
a blue sliver of cat eye, in temples of oak leaf,
with lips of echo or purring lion throat, kisses
of dragon flame or sibilant peaches, cunts of sea
snails in involutions of mother-of-pearl, milk
and honey nipples in each pore, nails of the moon
sparking on the hard stone, the smile they smile
upon this passing head alone, the glances of fire
upon that hand, that hand, that throat, glances
of aurora given to the sweet and salty tears
of the sea, sandpaper tongue, licking
their way through the finest hair, a thicket
of cat sighs and limbs of serpentile entwining, wild
berries prickled to ripeness by the falling
lip of fingerprint or taste bud, once human
too, born in maternal cream, wanting to be
as much as anyone else, driven by the desire
to be loved into human habitations, instead caught
as images of unrepentent injury in the net
of another's eye, changed into voiceless replications,
raptors of the banquet table, banished to cobweb
and spider's bite, leaving a kiss shyly upon
that ankle that kicks free of its heavy slumber,
its exhausted dreams thrashing limbs into
open air, a knot sleepwalking in the fetal
brain, until you wake, while looking in
a mirror, see you have given birth to
the chimaera that you are, the lovely, the lively-
locked, decomposing the self into some more
tangential music

X

Don't misunderstand, I'm glad you're well,
that the fever's left you, but we meet more
necessarily when we are sick. The nuns
who clustered around my childhood coma
seemed my soul's flock upon waking. My mouth,
kissed by nothingness, woke to another language.
Perhaps, as you said, every illness is the fragility
of the body opening into consciousness.
While you were ill, your name shrank to its
first letter, that *alpha* of identity, and you
said good-bye to me with three *x*'s, that letter
of sweat intersection—the linguistic root of suffering.
Now home again in pleasantry and distance,
these "warmly" and "best wishes" and every
"fare thee well" (though I thank you for each one),
at moments, I want back again—that dire gaze
of being, that *x,* its burning kiss.

Editorial Advice

So many words beggaring a reply,
but where does the mouth find its own

language?
Soul or heart, whatever

it is that tongues us into being,
original

because *originating.* So many
toddle babylike

between the spark and the wood, wanting
to warm their hands

on the fire they have not yet started;
so many

book jackets and spines calling out
for mother and father,

pushing their way headlong—premature infants
of the fetal word.

And one wants to say: go out and lie
"face downward

in the earth" or in the ashes of being,
anywhere

you can nest in the silence, until you feel
one real syllable

rising within you, as unmistakable and as prickly
as the eruption

of a new pinion feather
of a new wing

sprouting out of that so plucked, so
fucked-up nightingale.

Thieves of Fire

I'm slightly disturbed when my friend writes
that guilt made her take my books to bed, not
because I'm unmindful of the erotic
life of the word. I understand in the most
primitive way how the child eats the text,
which she is, and isn't that why Rousseau
argued, having learned the art of hand and mouth
in some fever of the page, for the burning
of all books? All those children who look into
their father's Bible for the breasts of the biblical
heroines on the illuminated page, as I read
my mother's novel of Alexander the Great,
which I was forbidden because his mother
entwined with Zeus's glowing serpent.
The tongue licks the finger that slowly turns
the page. It's the word *guilt* that bothers me,
for I think of guilt as nothing but pleasure,
thwarted or postponed, which can return to us
only disguised as obligation, and I don't want
her to take my books to bed out of obligation; I just
want her, *I just want her to be the snake in my bed.*

If this were a romance you were writing

Languishing in that exhausted bed
of stunned mullet and barely emergent
tendril, unable to write another word
of the wind or rain or winter you
cannot seem to wake up from, it was
the word you used, *siesta,*
that made me take up naps again, reminding
me of Spain, the long lunches of wine
and garlic chicken and a flock of wild
quail upon a plate, the almond dust
of Granada, that heavy languor
of afternoon, all the drowse of summer
heat, a dulcet grasp, invisible, so everywhere,
grasping soft being in its hand as lightly
as the sprig of rosemary upon a gypsy palm.
Some other tongue upon my tongue,
I went and dreamt of that, abandoned
character, conquistador, poet
who languishes as you do, and felt
so full of pity for his imprisonment
in your blank pages of the self (yours
or his, I could not say), so bored
and exhausted, the cries of *caquipas*
seem phantoms in the walls. A discourse,
dimly remembered, in some other
room, I heard you say, "Oh, of course,
he has my nose," and then I saw you,
upon my bed, in that real room where
I did sleep, the rose petals that you
sent me now dried to strange forms
of red and yellow, strung on that fine
blue thread, the same color as July
blueing all my windows—yes, in the

prison of myself—like gaps or *Leerstellen*
or seashells made transparent
and irregular by rub of wave or
butterflies with single wings stirring
in a rose and yellow cloud. Oh,
it was you, I saw you clearly (who never
see you but only feel your presence
in my dreams, though who's the phantom,
you or self, I cannot say)—the angle
of your cheek, your hazel eyes, that
dark hair brushed back around an ear,
as if a hand has just run through
and left it chaotic from the touch,
but mostly knew, by the nose,
yours, and his, some remnant
of Greek or Italian blood, some
ancient profile sculpted to pride or vanity,
yet lovely, slender, tender-tipped,
you leaned toward me without a word
and looked as fiercely as a hawk
might, disturbed above some
distant meadow, hearing some barely
audible call—the cry of parrots locked
in a wall, the blood imprisoned
in a pulse—then kissed me on the lips.

but it's a room of silent looms

I had rather be a kitten and cry mew
Than one of these same metre ballad-mongers.

Henry IV, III.i

No, he won't give up,
that dog humping your leg,
his pink engorgement
finding an invitation
in any casual contact.
Pat him on the head,
and that moist appendage
leaps forth, beading
with the sweat of its
own excitement as his
tongue laps at the air.
He thinks you're always
calling to him with your
scolding, your feet trying
discreetly to kick him aside,
and your desire to shovel him away,
just the inducement
to further exertions.
"Categories of gender," "the
complexities of being," is a woman in a room full of men
like a cat in a room full of dogs?

Next door, the girls are having
their own workshop; they are
naming their own breasts;
they are decorating the
interior of their own uteri;
the woman who no longer

has one, weeps; one girl
finds the voice that has been
asleep in her hands so disturbing
when it wakes up singing, that
she must leave the room.
They all invoke the voice
of the lost woman in their families,
all the buried women, the one who ran off
to live with the family of cats in the rosemary bushes, while in the next room,
a young man who is named for a saint who punished himself

for eating peaches is telling me
a story of a great bush of rosemary,
the herb has grown into a tree
at the university, and, according to
this Saint Augustine of the beautiful
mouth and the luxuriant beard, within its
dense fragrances, there is a family
of cats, and this reminds me… Oh
once, when I was a child,
this scroungy dog showed up and
stayed around our house for days
and days; we gave him away
finally because he was always trying
to hump the cats, he was the same size
they were; he seemed to think
it was nothing but a matter of size;
that they fit him in some way;
there was nothing we could do
to discourage him. "It's not really sexism." "It's just size."
"I have this habit of talking over every woman's head,"

because in their own rooms,
the women all have small voices;
they mumble to themselves among
the empty looms, where they are weaving

themselves together. Nothing is so
easily divisible into cats and dogs,
when one of them brings chalices
like communion cups and fills
them with beer and another brings
a loaf of bread as if it were the body
of a forgotten god, but then spreads
a garlic paste of almonds and olives
upon it. "What about issues of class?" "What about the fair dividing
of this loaf of bread?" "Don't you owe me some

money?" but in this room of silent looms,
who is the priest
and who is the servant? Who is
the lover and who is the friend?
And if this is a sort of communion
when one woman brings a loaf
of bread and chalices to another,
it is also a profane feast, for
when she wakes up in the middle
of the night, thinking of her work,
she'll drink all that's left of the sacred
wine and finish off the almond paste
and lick her fingers when she's done
as if she were a cat licking her whiskers, licking her paws,
smiling to herself, *my dear, my dear,* in the depths of the rosemary bush.

"The erotic is the spark in the tinder of knowing"

Oh, don't be afraid that we'll be lovers
and make a wreck of your life, for the truth is
we already are, yet you sit in your kitchen
each morning as usual, without me and
drinking your coffee, and those yellow roses
that I sent for your birthday are just what grace
I could rescue or steal from the meadows
of death and like my heart and the bones
of my body will surely wither and fade.
All this talk of the impossibility of being
lovers, all this fear and forswearing
of the body, all this being struck to the crow
clear space in the chest at three in the morning,
the tears that break the breath with pants of pain
or the tears that flow inaudible as mercy,
is just a way of making love. More difficult,
entwining in the bed of language, making
these tiny distinctions between ourselves
on the white sheer page like the spaces between
fingers that untwine only to clasp again,
more difficult, disrobing the self, to unveil
in knowing that interior nakedness
for which nothing has prepared us. That coil
around your heart is not just fear, but the lost
body of Eros in his original and beautiful
form, who stood in the middle of "chaos"
that meant then not a jumble of limbs but
openness, a clearing like a halcyon meadow
in a shady wood, creating an attraction between
all things—the galaxies of stars in the heavens
and the cells within your skin, and the letters
entwining into words, a corresponding
and adhering—whatever it is that makes us

come to that sweet numbness of the tongue,
each so alone in our benighted shattering and
articulating wound; whatever the soul is,
whatever the body, it's not just fear
that makes you quiver in that corner of that
most distant room of your life or yourself,
as if a word from me, traveling so far
out of the sea foam and the laughter of dolphins,
would undo the room, the ordinary table
and chairs, like a hand undoing the last
button on a dress before it falls to the floor.

According to the myth,

Love is for begetting and birth in the beautiful,
and the waters were *alumbramiento,*
their penumbra shedding glow, bringing the body
of light to the surface of the subterranean depths,

where I was floating in obscure of mind.
Everything quieted, every paradise in me
with its chattering parrots and tiger eyes
hushed with the palpable that had fallen upon me

like a pregnancy of meaning laboring to come forth,
and was not my heart with thee?
All being is pregnant, both in body and soul;
I was waiting, neither asleep nor awake,

poised at the edge of something, as if at the tip
of a nipple or tongue, waiting to speak
a dusky fire, flickering, *alumbrar,* to illuminate,
for beauty is the lady of labor, and when what is

pregnant comes near to a beautiful thing,
it becomes gracious and is poured out
at the hymen of being, where the beloved
awakens and puts on her skin like a gorgeous garment

and gives birth to an invisible child,
whose limbs are words, and who sings and sings
a song more blue and piercing
than the lost blue of the sea.

and I am the flower thief

who can't remember their varieties and names, speaking
in tongues among them, it was months before you,
months before I would smell you on my fingers, for hours
the yellow pollen of your sweet cunt, and perhaps that's all
I longed for in those deserted meadows and civic plazas
when I was a thief among the flowers. There were so many blooming
in the false dawn, each with a particular shape and a way
of wounding the fingers and intoxicating the lungs, the slice
of their bladelike leaves, the heavy heads full of rain,
the stamen and pistil in the deep-throated cups, the creamy
yellow stain of the corolla and calyx, the lips of the leaves,
artemisia, sea lavender, the blue monkshood, I knew only
the names adrift in the book, not attached to the world,
or what they were attached to, I was just learning to speak,
I was imitating Lorca in the cool drench of the dawn,
chanting *green, green, I want you green,* remembering
that moment, when watching love die upon a stage,
you plucked as if feverish at my white sleeve, I could have,
like Rimbaud, named them flora and taken them home to wither
on my mother's table, or like Baudelaire punished
une fleur for all the insolence of nature,
but I was just intoxicated, caught up in the meadows
that I carried in my arms. Years later, I would wonder
what had I done with them? all those fields of flowers?
I must have slipped them into some depth of water,
must have put them into some translucent vase or
someone's arms, but all I remember was being among
them, how the flowers, so freshly severed, felt in my arms,
how they moved against my lips, a drift of shifting color,
the touch of their petals brushing my cheeks, their stems
like the body of the rain against my skin, and the sense
of holding something that I could barely contain.

White of snow or white of page is not

the white of your skin, for skin, except
when truly albino, always has some other color
sleeping within it—a hint of red maple leaf,
a touch of the blue ice at the edge of a melting
stream, a richness implied of its many layers,
the deltas of cells and blood, that deep fecundity
that lies within and makes the skin shed, not
like a snake, but as a tree (one of those golden
cottonwoods flaring just now at the edge
of the river) that sheds its leaves each moment
while an eternity of leaf remains. Oh, nothing
seems to me as white as your skin, all your languid
ease of being—one resting upon the other,
the sliver of your shoulder against the black
fabric—reminds me so of the lost realm of beauty
that I am afraid of nothing, and only dazed
(as I was that day at the aquarium when the beluga
whales came swimming toward me—how white
they were, slipping out of the darkness, radiant
and buoyant as silence and snow, incandescent
as white fire, gliding through the weight of water,
and when they sang in that chamber as small
as the chambers of the human heart, murky
with exhaustion and captivity and the fragments
of what they had consumed, I was almost in love
with them; they seemed the lost children
of the moon, carrying in their milky mammalian skins
a hint of glacial ice and singing to each other
of all the existences they had left behind, their fins
like the wings of birds or angels, clicking and whistling
like canaries of the sea: *there was no darkness*
in their bodies, like clouds drifting through

unkempt skies, they illuminated the room).
So I did not think of you so much as I felt you
drifting through my being, in some gesture
that held me poised like a hummingbird above
the scarlet blossoms of the trumpet vine, I kissed you
above the heart, and by above I mean there,
not that geometric center, the breastbone
that so many use to divide the body in half and so mistake
for the place where the heart lies, but the exact
location, a little to the left, just on the crescent
where the breast begins to rise; oh, I know
all that drift of white implies, the vanished clothing,
the disappearing room, that landscape of the skin
and night that opens in imagination and in feeling
upon a sea of snow, so that just one kiss above
the heart is a kiss upon the heart, as if one could
kiss the very pulse of being, light upon the head
of that pin that pins us here, that tiny disk where
angels were once believed to dance, and all that
nakedness without could not have been
except for all that burning deep within

The Black Dress

It's flesh we love first—the angle of light upon
an arm, our earthly mouths to an earthly
breast—ourselves no more than a dim rocking,
our beings as small as a question mark dreaming
on a field of paper, into the word, the black dress
of the world that *she* puts on and strolls down distant
sidewalks, into a theater, a house, among the silverware,
and lifts the ebony cup of fire up to her earthly lips,
or chews ice. For it's flesh we love last—the angle
of shadow upon an arm, our earthly mouths to
the earth's breasts, ourselves *no more, no more.*

The Fragments of Hölderlin

The poor Hölderlin was taken away to
be brought back to his relatives.

Daily I must call upon the disappeared divinity

He made all efforts to escape.

If I think of great men, in great times, how they, holy with fire, transformed
*   themselves—all*
dead, wooden, as straw of the world—into flame, transformed

> now what can I do
> except watch you
> get dressed again,
> putting on all the
> distance of the world,
> the lost skin of the
> animal, full of the drift and
> cold

But the man who took care of him
pushed him back into the coach.

which flew up with them to the sky, and back to me,
but I go around often, glowing, like a small lamp begging for oil

> this room does not exist
> except in the house of my
> own being,
> full of many rooms,
> where I find you,
> a drift of soul
> nakedness,
> in a darkness that belongs
> to someone else

Hölderlin shouted

Oh, the marvelous showers me in quiet, but **"I" is the fright word,**
alive dead ones! You, that it lies.

what will I do with
you
now that all the veils
and the faces
have fallen away,
now that I've
forgotten
my own name,
then remembered it
and thought it
belonged to someone
else

that **Harschierers** are kidnapping him

(Do you lie?
humans are afraid before each other,
oh I am afraid before you)

and made more efforts. He scratched the man

the image of the hand began to glow,
on the left of its palm, a stain
like that of menstrual blood

with his enormously long fingernails

the other one who sites darkly over there, a shape upon a horse,
a hat pulled down upon its brow

into bloom, so thinking
her heart was on fire
as mine was, I leaned over

and kissed her cool stone
cheek, her eyes dreaming
into the sweet smile
of the closed lids that
only open within,
and felt for a moment,
wherever you are, in
whatever
world, I
was kissing you

For if it be meal and drink, but nothing that feeds the soul
If something that they say and do is understood,
Mental in the other one,
Transformed into flame.

absence is felt
so strongly
that the soul
tears itself
open:
how naked
you were,
dressing in front of me

what sort of god is this who arranges an infinite
number of details and lives, so that he can swat
out two lives like flies, or make certain
that we both fall from the tree of life
like two leaves, on opposite sides
of the world, as at the passing of an angel's wing

The Töerigen!!

and yet I might be mistaken
as when I thought I heard a sound like running
water, a stream of water splashing over stones,

and realized it was the golden leaves
of the cottonwood tree, rustling in the wind

> *As if possibly something that humans could say to each other*
> *would be more than firewood,*
> *which becomes only*
> *if it seized by the mental fire*

most often when I was with you, I was
neither awake nor asleep, but on
the threshold of some other being

> *Do you remember our unimpaired hours, where we and we only*
> *around*
> *each other were? That was* Triumpf!

                                                    (the dense
                                                    body of a
                                                    demon sitting
                                                    on my chest)

I never fill up with God or the wings of angels,
but you, in the most mundane things, how
you settle into a chair or put on your coat to go meekly
down the stairs toward dinner

> *to be so freely and proudly and awake and flowering and shining to*
> *Soul and heart and August and face,*

down that darkened road, the mountains do not resemble
breasts, and what's tempting about seeing the earth
as a woman, as if it were one's lover, is the scale—
for to see the earth that way, it is as if one would be
lying next to the beloved,
                        Next to each other!
to see the mountains thus, it would be
                    as if the earth loved us,

as if it were an intimate body that held us in its arms,
as flowers might be said to hold the hummingbirds
fluttering inches above the stamen and pistil,

>   when everything goes on
living in me, so when I've stepped out of that narrow
vessel of the self, that coffin, I keep moving, feeling
something within me moving still, even when I am
motionless, as if I were no more than a rising
>   or falling through the air

>   *at that time, being one already punished and said*

when I was a child and found a piece of petrified
wood, though I greatly desired to keep it,
I left it, and leaving it, felt I had it forever

I learned I could keep things forever
by giving them away

>   *One could probably wander through the world and would find it*
>   *hardly again in such a way*

so forever, I have that book with its pages like leaden wings,

>   *But a world can replace?*   but
>   who
>   could I
>   have
>   given
>   you
>   away
>   to?

I used to think I saw god in these clouds
in the sky,

We kissed ourselves—

broken open into storms and light,   *the*
                                      low-
                                      moved
                                      joyful
                                      soul on
                                      the
                                      lips—

and this "IS" makes my loyalty eternal
And in that and that one

                    many are splendid, but a nature, like
                    yours, where everything is
                            united in intimate, indestructible
              alive,
eternally lucky and eternally unfortunate

I move through the world as if I were nothing

THE BRIDLE

the burn that the oven rack scorched into

my hand last night dawns as a seal of umbra,
across my skin, a streak of slightly pregnant cloud
across a summer sky, or the slick track that a slug leaves,
all the fluidity of itself, a shining kiss upon the earth,
a part of me and yet apart, epidermal marvel
of how cells heal when the heart cannot,
so often, when we are burned by fire,
we become the waters that we are,
welling up between the injured
layers, the clear fluid of deepened thought,
as if what were dispersed within gathered
into that blister like a drop of rain, that palm
full of salty water, so that the hand cups
and tries to hold, clear and cool, the river
of its own being that gathers in every vein and cell, swelling
now and overflowing beneath the transparency
of the skin, where some touch has burned
too deep, how to grasp the truth of
what being is, without owning, without
being owned by, except a tactfulness
of feeling, fingers grasping with such
a delicacy of touch—the burning edge of all that is

Muse of Translation

"There is no muse of translation," the translator reminds
as he struggles with Pindar's victory odes, and what he means
is that the imagery is overwhelming: the hissing of snakes
as Medusa's sisters mourn her death, the baby Iamos
"lying on a bed of yellow and purple violets," Heracles
with his baby hands strangling the two serpents sent
"to devour him on the day of his birth" so every translator
must beware of "rank transplantation." Just imagine,
if one were to translate the line as "Forge your tongue
on the anvil of truth." How ridiculous that admonition
to a king. Better to transpose to the vague modern,
though Pindar "perversely, from our point of view—often
seems to relish... the concrete image," and it's just
there that I think perhaps all being is translation; the child
I was at the kitchen table, translating my mother into
my father, my father into my mother; each one's
"inviolate honey" becoming the "blameless venom"
of the other. So now I too prefer the naked tongue,
even pained and writing, caught in hammer and tongs,
flexed and torqued upon the anvil, until the metal
turns mercurial, quick, spilling into and out of
the shape of everything that is. For all day, while that pair
of grey-eyed serpents feeds the abandoned
child on honey, and the e-mail box fills with a multitude
of voices debating the distinctions of the hoaxes
of authorship—the pseudonym, the heteronym, all the masks
we can put on—I have trembled
because of my tongue. Because it insisted
upon saying *I love you.* So it waits and waits for some word from you.
It's late in the afternoon when you finally reply and then to the quote

I sent to a list. I read obliquely, wondering
if I should hope because you say you're thinking
of Shakespeare's sonnets (the beloved and the lover's love)
or if I'm lost to the shadows you're going off to dispel
with a cup of coffee, that "best" at the end
of your letter, my allotment from now on. Is it too much love
or too little that I have translated into being? Oh by now
I'm mistyping *forget* your tongue upon the anvil
that the tongue itself has made.

Isolate, you mean to be inviolable,

for, oh, it's not

the work of art I want to touch, though I did
that evening in that Fifth Avenue apartment when I'd moved
instinctively toward the wall, to get away
from the crush of people around the cocktail table
where the latest book by our hostess
was prominently displayed, and I found myself
looking down at that book by Keifer—open, its left pages arching
as if still moved by the touch of some vanished
hand, as if the paper had reached up into the air,
arching the spine beneath that stroke
and had not quite fallen down again into the binding.

The pages were rough, clotted drips
of grey and blue, and I think I remember knives
of pink or yellow. It seemed a book made of luminescence
though not lacking in knowledge of being extinguished, for
the page was a leaden wing lifting
in my hand. I could not help but touch it,
looking down into it, and yet as I describe
how I fell into it, my fingertips brushing
the ridges and pores of its skin, the capillaries
of its inscriptions, its smooth plane rising in my hand, it's you
touching with this art of flesh and blood, my body

turning beneath your palm,
as if I could, as if you would...

In an Atavistic Country

the earth is full of a thousand faces
a cliff resembles crocodile skin   a tree opens the eyes
of a leopard's skin   two shells lie side by side in the surge
of whatever washed them together   it is the land of *yes*
another country   where the dragons are small
and bask in any shining   their toes splayed out in ecstasy
as the warm air makes their own blood flow faster,
slipping in and out of torpid shadows   quick tongues
speaking of dust and silence   so the imagination
has such delicacy   it hovers at the edge of the grass
and waits for the arrival   *oh breath held back*
of the tiny emperors   full of spikes and crowns

There is no garden here,

just the pale hooks
of the foxtails, which, snagged in the skin
of dog or goat, sometimes begin migrating
into the torso's interior, penetrating
the vital organs—for what is the flesh
for a seed but a kind of earth?—and so
become an internal ache in what we think
of as the self, that cyst, sealed by self-defense
between subcutaneal layers, sometimes
a pocket of infection that distorts
the smooth delineation of the limbs, as a face
may be so gouged by look or word
that it is plowed around the eyes, and yet
standing at night beneath the half-moon
the foxtails seem the silvery hair of all
that light, so beautiful in intricacies
of tuff and stem, my eye falls upon them
as if my gaze were the touch of a lover's
hand, for the garden in all its ruin (the dog
has chewed up the white cross the children
placed to mark the death of another beloved
pet), luxuriant green and rich flowers stripped away
by drought, a bramble of weed along
the fence, at night when I go out
and drowse in it, seems but my ruined self,
where I debate whether to take up the shovel
again, to plant new bulbs, to scrape
the earth and pull up weeds, their roots
tearing free with a satisfaction I never feel
in weeding out myself, the dirt under
my fingernails—oh, to try and make it
a paradise again—or just give up and leave it
to another and become a gypsy like the moon.

At first the blank stare I met in the garden only
broke me into tears, and, now in some altered
state in which my altering mind becomes
oddly more "me," I have these conversations
with the night's black gaze of being,
while above me, clouds drift past
the moon. Last night there was but one great cloud,
a drifting thing that passed across the sky like
a wave that pulses over sand; it swept so slowly
across the nocturnal, it could have been a lover's
hand that turned to dark only to touch, for
as it drew nearer to the moon and became
a grasp of light, the cloud became a pale burning,
a broken halo around the moon, as if wherever
the moonlight touched, it turned the nimbus
the color of wildflower honey or amber,
which was believed a remnant of the goddess
dismembered and fallen to earth:
a translucent pale gold like that treasure
found only in the skin of living things,
petals or the fins of fishes or the flashing
wing feathers or like a forearm
taking on the color of lions in the first
light of summer, or the golden carp in the overcast
eye of a pond. The cloud seemed some
animal of indeterminate and vague shape,
always becoming, always breaking apart,
translucent as those glass fish one can see
through, as if in looking at it, I could see
through to the other side of all Dark,
that threshold of being within oneself.
A kind of creature of the air, it poured
itself through all that was obscure, its moving
like a kind of music, which I following
began to feel pouring through myself,
and so this morning, stripped of bewitching and cloud

and moon, it came to me, in wreck of garden,
that we are just the dragon's children,
bearers of the earth's lost song that pours
through us like drift of cloud across the sky,
caught on the very edge of being
in all the ruin we have made.

Tree of Words

Oh, I'm scanning and cropping all these photos,
to isolate the distinguished writer, the illustrious
head, so the viewer won't know this lyric young man
was actually arm-wrestling when he was caught
in sleepy smile or that this epic poet was hedged
by young girls with bouquets, too distracted to notice,
staring as he was into the invisible depths of that sadness
lapping at his feet. It's instructive what's edited out:
for instance, girlfriends or wives, with or without floral
arrangements, the tables covered with beer steins
and cigarettes, the odd folklore motif on the ceiling
of two village girls, upside down, at either end
of a lumberman's saw. Little by little, world
and woman is scissored out, until nothing is left but the black-
and-white elegy, the enigma of the poet's sadness,
which he broods upon like a goose trying to hatch
a robin's egg. But, oh, on the wall
that I was deleting, in the lovely dendritic of green,
among the airiest of branches, there's a goat
perched in a tree! I used to see that daring rapture
on the faces of our goats, the kids perched lightly
on their mothers' backs: a certainty of balancing
on nothing, of being firmly footed in air.
Surely, that's the soul's way, a kind
of delicacy perched upon the thinnest of branches
that neither bends nor breaks. But the goat's not
the soul of poetry, nor the cipher that the world becomes
upon the mind's back wall, but something else
that we can barely name, though she calls and calls
us to her paradise—that imaginary tree.

After John Donne's "The Dreame"

Now do all my metaphors break. Yet still
I err with these sweet names: of bee, of hive,
or honeycomb, *o sweetheart, o honey, my dear.*
Each metaphor bears a distortion—its gaze but
a facet of a dragonfly's stereoscopic eye—
and a wound—the deer that leaps when the arrow flies,
the iron deep into the flesh—that makes love,
even divinely met, a wounding and a mortal
pain, of consuming and of being consumed,
when what the heart most longs for is an end
to all these songs of predator and prey.
To dwell in some other paradisiacal *o you*
where, beyond all *Feare, Shame, Honor,*
one wakes not to wonder if "Thou art not thou,"
but to bear the wonder of all being, where I
am I and you are you and love but is and is.

Salt River

In many languages those ancient explorers
named the mountains for breasts—how egocentric
and how lonely! Yet I think, descending
this mountain pass at night, where at least one
clearly delineated hill has its small nipple
in the mouth of the full moon, what's tempting
about seeing the earth as a woman is revealed
by the scale: to see the mountain as a breast,
one would have to be lying next to the beloved,
would have to have one's lips just inches from
her nipple. To see the mountains thus
would be the most intimate existence, as if
the earth loved us and took us in her arms,
as flowers might be said to hold the hummingbirds
fluttering, suspended, inches above the stamen
and pistil. As if the stillness that is born of
the unceasing movement of one's desire
and the pull of gravity, always insisting upon
a conclusion, were an embrace meant for each
of us. When in truth, everything moving within
us goes on moving, it's like the motion of falling
or rising through the air in an elevator or speeding
down the descending curves of the earth's body
as I am, at eighty miles per hour. Once one has
stepped out of the narrow vessel of the self,
that coffin and its consummations, what was fluid
goes on flowing, not a human form fashioned out
of salt, but a river of salt—all that dizziness of the real
where the self cannot keep anything, even by giving it away.

On the Island of Bones

Predictably,

    For the wound did not begin with us:

my left temple throbs

    the first Europeans found this island scattered with bones—

as if a scavenger bird
had sat on my shoulder, all night,

    cayo de hueso,

trying
to eat its way into the most intimate spaces

    connected to the continent by a ligature of reef,

of my self, its claws so grasping

    a siren shore to those explorers—their desire and their fear—

(though I could call it my *harpy* husband), into the interstices of my
    muscles,

    full of the enchantments of erasure,

that I seem the bruise
of his insistence,

    so many shreds and wounds of meaning

that I can barely look
through the white sheer panel that veils
the sea

    "the poet
    looks at the world as a man looks at a woman,"

round eye, round island,

     and so they found the shining mirror of the sea

but I am not a man, so have to look at the ocean as if I,

       by following the lines they'd memorized

as if I,
as if I existed, as if *I am*

     the word *cayo* altering on many lips

and so my fingers are as gentle and as hesitant

     into a word that in another language

as if I touched the wound in you

     sounded like the word for key—

swimming into the blue of the water, the body of the world

     oh mastery, of signs of doors of maps—and made the world

and something within me

     into a graveyard

rising from dead—

     where once was paradise.

oh yes, it's paradise!

For, yes, I think that form inflicts a kind of violence,
perhaps the repetitive step of the *iamb,* that girl (I am)
for whom it was named in every Greek tragedy,

the one whose cry interrupts everything,
     enchanted, or in pain…

was caused by the shackles upon her shins,

> Oh I remember those women waiting outside
> the gate of the Alhambra (always waiting *outside*
> the gates) to capture me with the weight
> of sprig of rosemary they placed upon my open palm

though perhaps the apologists are right (I don't
think so) and she wore nothing but the finest gold chain
of privilege.

> as if to captivate with intricate *o verde*
> *te quiero verde,* my walking through the world
> a drowsy somnabulist, full of the almond dust of Granada.

Perhaps there was no other way for her
to move, and what we call order is a wounding,
like hobbled horses in a meadow, a dragonfly tied
upon a string, for I am thinking, the body of the ocean

> Yet, you could not know
> when you sent me this charm of the Gypsies,
> how I would cast it, I could stand in the aureole of any
> candle and say to any you—

outside my room is so fluidly and chaotically
beautiful, the light so random and impending,

> *warmth of heart and passion fire, to be blessed*
> *by the heavens is our desire—*

that I feel nothing can correspond to it except
except my feeling for *you,*

> though it would always be I,
> full of the crushed petals of that flower
> Eros gave the god of silence, like drops of blood
> my slightly cut finger left upon the floor.

for depth and subtlety
of feeling, and how can one ever write the idea of order?

       Oh, they wanted me to cross their palms with silver
       and have my fortune read.

It's like thinking of the anchorite's penance
or the flagellant's whip, while daydreaming
in the arms of the beloved.

       A clay heart, a spell of fire, a feather,
       and a taste of the magick potion
       like salt upon the tongue.

O beloved, I keep thinking
some other idea is needed, I keep waking to the impossible

       A talisman of terra cotta, a child's toy, a game,
       incised with a symbol
       that is one shape or is two:

hour, at the very moment, the obscure body of the night
begins to fill with impending light,

       inverted cross that rises out of an x
       but, viewed if framed by the heart shape,
       an x rooted in the earth

when the depths
are no longer mistaken for the cold compression,
the vacuity that we have made them, and the *I,*
having adjusted to the shades of its absence,

       and flaring out of its rising stem
       could be a child's depiction of a flower,

as the eye adjusts
to perceive the phosphorescent and transparent forms
of the fish that thrive within the depths,

for the spell you sent me is the spell already cast.

 Underwater, vents of volcanic steam
surrounded by the waving meadow of sea worms, the brain coral
in its aquamarine electric halo that seems to think in bodily terms,
 so that its many creatures form one green continuous thread,
 a kind of unraveling nimbus, and each creature is so rarely formed,
 that I marvel at it as if it were the unique body of the beloved,
O you, it's only you, that freckle on your arm, each creature bearing
its own radiance upon its head, a hook, a lantern, a shimmering veil...

 With the innocence of sharks resting together
 in the waters, if I sat in midnight and watched the water
 move, I could not write these words,
 which abide in the dark and watch
 the water move, you who are evening,
 you are dusk, you who are every hour,
 singing to me in some constant or inconstant tone,

for in this world I want nothing but you, and the round eye of the moon
looks to me as if it were sick of all the stories it has been made to bear,
and the seabirds that dive and arc over the water each morning are silent,
though they make of themselves a weaving, whatever sound they make
is the sound of wind, the sound of wave, we try to cast a spell upon...

 Who could sail these waters, so hanged
 with sun and blue, the delicacies of these breezes,
 and land upon this shore of serrated leaf
 and black-ringed dove and plant a cross and a gallows,
 two shapes of order and inquisition, and architect the shadow
 of what we mistake for passion upon the living mangrove islands
where the nurse sharks lie in basking herds, their brown and blond coiled
ease in the blue shallows, a nestling of shape and length, where the trees
 themselves are so rooted, extending into coral, each rootlet
 finding the way in, and so entwined, that in their knotted hands,
 the earth itself is caught, all the dust blown by the wind, debris

of leaves and scattered shell, and so the land takes form in that embrace,
so multicelled and polyformed, that the coral glows with the electricity
of its own being and wears the veils once attributed to the divine body
of the goddess, the veil that draped the rioting hair of the woman saint
so she could enter church and not disturb those praying with
the protean quality of her hair or thought, and the anemones in their long
and jointless swaying seem part grass, part wind, and mostly finger,
so swaying back and forth through the currents, so that being seems
to caress itself, while outside the most expensive window a plastic heron
with its open crook of neck planted on the top of some beach house
has replaced the gallows and the pontifical scepter at the top of the beach
umbrella, its toothed crown above the collappased (yes, I've misspelled
that but leave it, let language bear its own ruin) glaucous width
of the parasol has replaced the shadow of the cross, its implication
of miter, and the gunship that goes by full of tourists, full of blanks,
though out there beyond our sight, we know the actual
vessel of war carries its red crosses
and guns full of live (death-dealing) ammunition

He said that he thought his poem was about another kind of col-
onization of the mind but when he went past and cast his look
like a net upon the tall blond woman I was talking to, someone
else's wife who looked like his wife, I understood that he did not
mind the other forms of colonization, that he was speaking as a
man who had been deprived of the prerogatives of men, all that
European pride in a history that pained him, how he'd gone back
again and again to Italy trying to resist its seducation, it was
really sort of laborious, someone had said earlier that writing
poetry was like flying through concrete but I had the feeling I was
watching a man turn into a monument of himself, cell by self the
aggregation of authority and celebrity, until there would be a sun-
basted statue with his name upon it in some square, ponderous
with the details of the tourist, which came alive when it stirred for
a moment with something like anger, remembering how "with
this prodigious ambition one begins."

They were so lovely, so generous
arriving in their canoes to weigh
us down with fruits and flowers
and the sweet warmth of themselves

and I knew by this they would be fit
for servitude, so sweetly obedient
they already were, even to the gentlest breezes
of their paradise, that they

did bend and sway, like the
anemones who in those shallow
depths do swirl and move, opening and closing
like the hands of women, caught in another's tide,

angels, they seemed, in kindness, but bodily enough,
being no more than human,
their qualities of being angelic so
marked them out as slaves

that it seemed to me, those first manacles
were but the bracelets to anchor
them to this earth, which we must
make groan with our labor and our discipline

of gold and emeralds and all the
salts and spices that alone can make
life palatable to us, its penance become
many piercing flavors expiring on an exhausted tongue,

and so I leashed them, as once in my native country,
when I was a boy, I tied great-eyed iridescent
dragonflies to filaments of
string and watched them fly

back and forth, all morning,
while my mother's laundry dried
on the line, until their wings

tore off as their hearts failed.

I thought the heron, its neck crooked
so that the beak angeled (I meant to say angled)
at forty-five degrees into the air, as if the air
were water, as if all being were an ocean
where the heron fished, was real. But it was not.
As I saw only when I drew nearer to the world that seemed
so framed by my expensive view—the sheer drapes,
the plastic solar-blocking panels, the frame of window,
the frame of doors, opening onto the balcony with
its frame of wrought iron, for when I drew nearer
I saw the heron was equally fixed. It too was
part of the frame, architecture of the *I,* so that the Atlantic
blued by the sun would be caught in the angle of its motionless neck;
so do we try to still the world, to make it rest in lyric
and obey, thinking that it floats like water upon the eye of God,
and try to find in ourselves some equivalent moment
of dazzling and fixed stillness, and mistake it for what
we call peace. Yet we make a corpse of world and self,
banish real herons and bring in their disposable replicas
and posited signs, and then try to benedict the corpse
back into breathing. Farther on, I saw that the man
who had been standing on the concrete dock looking into the water
(I'd mistaken him for a homeless guy) was not alone. I had been all wrong
                                             from the beginning.
Another man was in the ocean, beneath the framework of the dock, at work
        upon something, in his T-shirt and jeans, I knew he probably floated
                in some raft or skiff bobbing there to reach the dock's
                        underside, but from my vantage,
                it seemed he had stepped into the water,
                his arms over his head reaching with great effort
        to hold up the dock, the underbelly of the world, a ceiling
                that pinned him in a world of waves and tossed him,
                        in the ceaselessly moving water.

So the evolutionary poet is rare. In actuality, it seems to me, many of my contemporaries are niche exploiters, each one attaching itself to some crevice of the reef to make a feast of whatever predictable scrap drifts its way. At dinner, thinking this, I became too feral, I think, in some conversation, I said something to the effect that no matter how complicated my view, I always read a poem as if it were a matter of life and death, that I was usually disappointed, that the evolutionary poet was rare, and whatever it was I said, it made one woman go off and burst into tears and made the other attending poet disappear into another corner to begin another conversation as firefighters might ignite a backfire to try and stop the forest fire that threatens to consume a picturesque town in the mountains. Later, this same poet came back and suggested that I was drunk, so I laughed, and said, no, at this stage of my life, I didn't need to drink to be intoxicated. Doesn't anyone notice that the great poet is simply a stricken bird? Though his missing teeth, the gap of his smile that suggests a twisted beak make me feel better about him: all poets should have a touch of the monstrous. But he is only celebrity, not that rare one who can barely breathe between the land and the sea, who moves not knowing if fins are fins or wings or hands, who finds these selves, who can she be who is herself and her own muse, who can she be but *you*, so easily confused in all her fluid swelling with the murk and mud of being?

In absolute statements
poetry perishes

Empathetic imagination
when required
makes one fill up with the dead

The distinguished hand
is frigid
as if it were the hand of a corpse
dreaded (dredged!)
up from the sea

                    Ah, it's the feral
            that interests me, the animals
            in the room, like the feral cat
            and chicken in almost any yard:

                                        that poet, for instance,
                                            who has the eye
                                        of a living possum
                            caught in the shine of a flashlight
                                    in the branches of a tree
                                        on the remotest hill
                            of an Arkansas back road.

Any paradise becomes too quickly swindled
and expensive, so when his charge-card machine
doesn't work, and I have no cash with which to pay
him, the British guy at the Internet café begins
to endure a kind of torment between his desire
to trust me, and his fear that I'll stiff him out
of the seventeen dollars that I owe him just
for talking to you, and his anxiety becomes
a grey upon his face, some cement of reluctance
in which his faith in another tries to rise, though
there's no help for it, since I have no money I can give,
so it's hopelessness that he gives into, having no choice
but to trust is not a choice to trust. Perhaps he senses
in himself the way in which I'm lying, for I do have
a twenty in my pocket, though it's all my son and I
have to eat on for the next two days, until the money
I've been expecting finally arrives, and perhaps
it's some deeper current between us, some way of knowing
what he cannot know, that makes it more difficult
for him to trust me. So when I come back in the next day,
new money having arrived, he's sitting outside on break
in the lounge chair, in a drift of dreams between customers
and when he sees me coming back to pay, oh how he smiles,
oh luv, he calls out to me, as if this paradise, real estated

and pirated into limbo, were paradise again, though
in a different way, for being merely human, for all our faltering
and our lies, some hovering shape in the air around us,
our selves opening, as if we were free

        snaggly toothed guy who plays songs
          requested on his violin,

          guy who spray-paints
      himself in warship grey and stands motionless on a corner,

  young girl who paints a plate with a place-name, the obligatory
        palm tree and wave of water,

        middle-aged fatso who'll tell
        a dirty joke for fifty cents,

     ex-hippie who has a parrot ride on his
     dog's back while the dog wears sunglasses,

   young woman, her face fainted white and fluttering
  dress and feathers of a Victorian angel in an elaborate
        pantomime,

     pleading to heaven, scraping gratitude,
elaborate over the amount of money dropped into a tin, it's all the racket
      of teeth chattering together,

   showtime for those couples who come down the gangplanks
  of the cruise ships like lumbering animal couples of an ark gone wrong,
  filled with replicas of the same species—hippopotami, shrewd
       weasels,

so when the boy sitting on the curb shouts to the sleepwalking couples
who clot up the sidewalk with the maneuvering of their rumps,
those whose eyes are fixed on some invisible
and distant horizon by all that they have drunk, he cries out

we don't want anything, we have what we need

and he means by this the sandwich that his hands are still full of,
its brown bread and overflowing lettuce and turkey, as if
it were the plenty of the earth itself, a kind of cornucopia,

we don't want your money, all we want is a little acknowledgment here

I look at him and smile and say *hello* and ask *how are you*
he says *fine, how about you,* and our eyes are equal,
so fixed upon each other, until the drift bears me away,

how are you, how are you, how are you

> In land's end bight
> all the ships were tied,
> the replicas of sailing ships,
>
> the turtle kraal
> images of slaughtered turtles
> and only one very small living turtle,
> a female with an injured fin, floating in the rescue tank
> just inside the door, and outside, the ocean too
>
> is full of junk, the scattering
> of seaweed like burnt straw upon the water,
> a dead pelican, its head folded into the water, and
> a small moon jellyfish, which at first
> I took for a plastic bag and then
> seemed dead but then my son
>
> threw a pebble into the water, and at the sound
> of threat, the jellyfish pulsed
> and began filling itself up with water
> and contracting frantically to get away,
> so hard for a creature, made of water,
> to make a way through water, for its road
> was *everywhere*, and as it pulsed
> and quieted, letting itself relax back into

                  its drifting, it moved with the muscular contractions
                  of the human heart that does not move in linear ways
                  but drifts and is taken and pauses and stops
                  and can only open or close

as a dream that lapped as the water does
at the *labia* of every form

for what is it,
should I say it's the muse, for all that it brings me
is the page trembling upon that pirate chest,
which has been turned into a piece of decorative furniture
in this expensive room, a page torn between the wind
that lifts it like a wing and the force of gravity that
makes it press against the surface of whatever
it rests upon, or perhaps more realistically it is the phantom
of my own desire that shapes out of nothing but its dreaming self
and nerve endings, all the cells opening to the night as the anemones
open to the water, caught in the longing for what they are not,
for in that sense, every Helen is a phantom, dreaming in her Egypt,
and if so, why call it *you,* why not give it the more easily defined
shape of the body dancing on that corner or the one who
will show me her breasts though I do not want her to, or the one who
says laughing my eyes are like *chispas,* those sparks
rise into the air though they are full of fire, as if they
might take flight, and yet it is you and your words that wake me,
not in your voice, for I don't know what your voice sounds like,
and so cannot hear it, even in a dream, it was just the words themselves
that were embodied, a kind of presence with gravity, and subtlety
of feeling, the wind, the weight, I don't know how, and so it's odd
how I wake up as if you had just spoken to me, the dead of night
beginning to fill with the impending glow, just where and how
do I live, what is the location of the soul, and does it
ever have an ordinary address, *for I am no one's, if I am not
yours,* for it seems to me, when your dreaming body lies in my dreaming

arms, that I held you, most truly you, that body which the Tibetans
believe walks out of the corpse after death and goes on craving
cigars and candy, it seems to me *so you* that I could believe you dreamt
your way to me as I was dreaming you.

Oh please, give me a break, the truth is, O phantom, form of the uncanny,
the correspondence of word and tongue, the silken form in all the depths,
that serpent's labyrinth of being, I'm sitting here listening to the song of
how I am amazed, but the truth is if you were in the next room, I'd be
rushing into you, perhaps slowly as a fish snagged by the hooks of its own
desire, being reeled in by myself, but rushing into you, like the breath
breathing from my lungs, I could not not this minute touch you, I could
not not kiss you, I could not not have my fingers in you, I could not not
be this vulnerability of you or me, the world itself would fall to the floor
like the last article of clothing, there's no heaven I would not give up to
enter you, I could not not touch the tips of my wings, my fingers, my
tongue, my nose, to the tips of your tongue, your fingers, your eyes, your
nose, your, I could not not be, could not not be yours, could not not be

how can the body remember what it does not know?
what phantom wakes me at night to the unknown
feeling of your body, my chin tucked into your neck,
my hand cupping your breast, a dove dreaming in my dreamt hand,

so that I wake to this real room, where, while I slept,
a drift of turning fan and rising wind has turned my notebook
to a blank page that, restless, flutters up on its spine,
vibrando, with its white space, its blue lines,

as if with love, as if to rise,
trembling with the impending sense of the impending
of the note there, as if in some phantom embrace
(I meant to write only "embrace" but let the word
remember) it felt the sea surging beyond the window,

its black rhythm rushing around the shores
to which it is bound, as if the ocean were that ancient river,
a phantom nestling against the back of the earth,
a serpent of desire encircling the world

why do these gestures inhabit us?
why did I wake up thinking of my tongue running
like a quick snail along your side, that side
that if you were a creature made of water

would be your dorsal side, if people were fish,
from hip to arm, so that I could taste the subtle
saltiness of you, as if the dream brought to me
the faint flavor of all the ocean outside my window,

the salt of your most distant molecule
to my most distant tongue
that intimate space where paradise lost
begins

THE FIRE

she invents

for me an angel bed,
with no bedposts, her love
for me is so archaic, it floats suspended there,
without bedposts or means of attachment,
wholly supported on *wish* alone, as she
waves it with a wand into my house,
that dark blue canopy embroidered
with gold and silver stars, like the chapel
where she often went to pray, its wooden ceiling,
an ancient map of heaven, so I might sleep
(I cannot sleep, I wake to *want's* empty stare)
upon its mattress and its pillows as soft as vapours,
and if that's not enough, she wishes me
a room full of lilies, so pure in fragrance
and in hue that I might believe I wake
to her, so sweet is her imagination; yet
it's all a dream like any dream, she cannot
wave a wand and wish herself here, nor am I
good or pure or true but only in and of my body
like that vase wherein the stems turn green and begin to rot
as the lilies fade, for all day I have heard the breeze
bearing from faraway, the distant rustling,
the low moans, of her making love
to *Him* in ordinary skin
and sweat upon a real, an earthen, bed.

The Shearing

Each hour they grow fewer, the splayed
lipped, white drift of the apple blossoms
falling to wind, late frost, and 90 lumens
of the brilliance of paper falling, shredded
to the floor, even incised with the black burning
of someone else's sacred defoliation, love is not
transitory enough but snail-like shapes
self to shell, or hooks like scorpion tail
in crevice or niche, long past luck or life.
Who wants to love forever? Love should fall
like the apple blossoms, die at the kiss
of a bee, learn to perish, come to an end.

"Fiction Weaving"

The *Encyclopaedia Britannica* has given *lesbianism* its own listing for the
first time in its 334 years of publication. The newly released 2002 edition
defines lesbianism as "the quality or state of intense emotional and usual-
ly erotic attraction of a woman to another woman."

In 1867,
    In a room full of looms
a medical journal article "The Influence of the Sewing Machine on
                           Female Health"
    We are weaving ourselves together
claimed that seamstresses were apt to become sexually excited
    "Female homosexuality does not exist," the Red Queen says,
by the steady rhythm of a sewing machine.
    "We don't need to ban what doesn't exist… Banning sewing
                     machines is another matter."
It was believed inadvertent orgasms often resulted from the up-and-down
                     motion

> *it's the lover*
> *in you who takes my bitten*
> *hand in your two hands, and it's*
> *the daughter in you who tells*
> *me to stop biting my nails*
> *annoyed in a public place*
> *by the sound of my animal*
> *tearing its own cuticles,*
> *snapping off its nails, and it's*
> *the mother in you who mourns*
> *over my hand*

of women's legs while turning the foot pedal.

It was suggested that to prevent this labor companies should
put bromide, a chemical thought
to inhibit sexual desire,
　　　　oh, the poor thing does deserve better,
into the women's drinking water.
　　　　　　　　　　　this room full of looms that have fallen so still
It was also stated that supervisors should circulate
　　　　among the seamstresses
　　　　　　　their threads like tongues
that have not yet knotted themselves into words,
so many selves, sewing ourselves into one, one each, one many,

to see who was sewing too fast.

　　　　Oh, in the elevator, on the stairs, on the snow-covered roof,
　　　　in the laundry room, on the bed, behind the bed, under the bed,
　　　　on the floor, those kisses
weaving themselves
together,
　　　　each our own tapestry in each other's

　　　　　　mistress
　　　　　　in her who leans into my hair
　　　　　　poet in her who enters
　　　　　　my ear, sister
　　　　　　in her that instructs my hand
　　　　　　to color, aunt in her
　　　　　　who remembers

　　　　fingers and fingers flying over lavender threads

among all the mysterious
fingerings,
　　　　(oh, "inadvertent" orgasms are the most dangerous kind)

　　　　　　love is a fiction weaving
　　　　　　into my palm, into yours

so many *you*'s, so many *I*'s,
                        snarled, raveling, unraveling
selves
borne upon
the surface of water, the current
of the flesh, a red maple leaf, a cunt, fragrant
as the dahlia, mysterious as the third eye in the dreaming
flesh, a discarded dress, the color of mourning, flowers
plucked from a meadow and set adrift, a blue parrot's
feather, a storm of butterflies, tiny
stones or obsidian tears or
caught in the drift or a turning in the eddies,
the pine needles, the childhood forest, or
the fingertips sticky with sap from
the ponderosa pine still smelling
of butterscotch

        what is most wonderful about a woman is the taste of her,
all parts of her,
                honey, amber, a cloved lemon, oyster tears
the petals of wildflowers, the eating of clouds, rain in their pores, wild
        raspberries,
strawberries, smoky flesh of small clams,
                "Lesbianism is a state of mind whose sexual organ
        is the skin,"
a quality, a state of feeling
                pores of echo
        in the cloud of skin,

my dear chestnut gatherer,
margery, molly, invert, unisexual, androphile, normosexual, parisexual,
        ghaselig, Uranian,
bigirl, doubling double, or in Turkish off-color terms
presbitorean (prehs-beh-toh-reh-yahn)
—for someone who writes erotic poetry
or pteronofili (peh-teh-roh-noh-fee-lee)

—taking sexual pleasure from being caressed with a feather
in… into… inadvertent, unmeant, unintended…

        animal
or any other
kindofmiraculous
blooming

in this room full of women and looms

Stuck on the Roof

how clotted in the choked throat, the nightmare
phones hang an abyss, a real one rings in curses,
how hard it is to fly away, all money fisted
in one grasp, the borrowings of pennies,
the infinitude of boxes, and even
the cage door creaking open
moments such a feral rage,
yet overwrought and paralyzed
no world believed in beyond wire,
and yet it's always the same choice, to gutter
out in sweat and welt, to turn as savage
as keepers are, or to surrender
in sweltering summer heat,
an animal run to ground, being torn
apart from within, as if something were
emerging, tearing out, through one's skin,
and yet it's always the same choice,
to climb the roof for the third time,
because that ancient plastic tubing cracks
predictably, but at random, as does the
not yet vanished fitting,
to be split thrice, to climb the slant
and scramble perch, precarious as top rung,
and fix it again, again, again,
to notice always the other door, that sky
that opens its blue petals, its softly scented animal
mouth, and looks all the way
to vanished kingdoms, horizons of unpeopled ruins
and ruined seas, for miles and miles through
terre verte bouquets of elms and cottonwoods,
and smiles its cloud bank along the eastern
horizon, and freshens with rain that may not arrive,
that makes it cool enough to lie here, ruffling

hair against burning tiles, that threshold of,
oh, tranquil being, those clouds so cirrus, delicate
fingerings whitening across blue, thinning
to sunbeam and air, featherings of Japanese orioles
and white Asian lilies, oh scale through which
the eye flies, oh sea in which the eye plunges,
to burn for love, the world does burn, *oh laugh,*

> *oh immanent in leaves or*
> *ashes and all the pores of*
> *living skin*

after two years, you say only
the British have a cultural sense of tact which is necessary
to "true intimacy," and I am not British, so

I have no tact

so balanced on my lips and fingers to touch
upon your skin, that knows

how to touch your invisible feeling, those tears beneath your skin.

   Whether asleep or awake,

my words fall upon your pulse
with a wincing weight,
so fumble fingered or glass shattering

and that sometimes sliver that rankles, so far beneath the nail.

      O tact—I have no sense
of you, my lost sense
of the senses, once measured among
         auditus, gustus, odoratus
like a living species of bee: in all that lightning
of the taste buds, all that fire
    on the tongue

of crushed pods
of burning seasons,
         the nose's delicate
intertwining
with filaments of scent,
         the whorls of the ears catching in their intricate coils
the membranes trembling in seawaves of sound,
                                             or

could have heard
the pain in you that made you breathless

in your sleep, and how you winced
    awake. I wish I spoke
some other language
of moon cognates
        and warming verbs, to make that tragedy
I have given you
        a comedy of bees
that enter, innocently, the meadowy sex
                                        of orchids,

    until the mind's only
    divine with dizzy
    starlight
so many selves within our cells. If I were tactful,
I might have heard what
        you could not say
all the damp extinguishment
                                    of being,

your tears of char
at trying to stub
out that burning brand
        in your aortal flesh,
those tears go mute, are never shed, they sting
the most lidded eye. You might never have thought it fatal
to open the pages of the subtleties of angels, all that light breaking

        the *I* open with desert architectures
of blossoms and thorns
        or mistaken yourself
for an empty spiral
beneath a beaded mask,
if I could have been some other language, perhaps a lullaby
        in French,
a Gypsy canto
        lilting by your window on a summer's night, so tactful
it might have seemed the body's anonymous song,

overheard, in passing, as if meant
for anyone else, I might have been

as tactful
          as tongue of bee is to what it penetrates and tastes,
as nimble as the body
          of feeling is with its eyelashes that lightly brush
through empty air. Would have abandoned the verbs
          for *see* and *know*
and been so touched
and touching,
          that as the desert opens
at the dew,
          you could have been that slowest snail
that fills up with the rain
          that fell like kisses so long ago, so tactful
with its slow going
over stones, that in the silver moisture of its track,
          the meadow itself would have seemed
to shimmer
          like angels giving birth to laughter.

When the universe looks into the eye, its gaze

is black water, no, not even
water, but blackness itself
for even the smallest and murkiest pond
has its water lilies with their pink clitoral buds
opening into creamy petals and the thick dust
of yellow pollen, the roots of the lilies
in their hairlike profusions knotting
the thick clay of the depths to themselves
as those pale and naked fingers begin
to break open what contains them
and proliferate across the waters
until on every surface, flat green palms
float like gentle hands above
the flash of the fugitive fish,
who leave only the traces
of gold scale and silver fin
as they appear and disappear
from view. The eye
of the universe is so devoid
of fugitive dazzle, so void
of variations in its shades
of bafflement, there is no ground to stand
upon and no air to breathe. All
that can meet the abyss without
is the abyss within, an absence
so forceful in its absence,
it seems more present than any presence,
and how does the *I* look back, or what eye
is left to return that gaze, when you are gone
how do I make upon these waters
a floating island, a lily hand,
a beckoning of light and fire?

Unknowing

whether I should say
     weather
of two orchids
          or one,
so dual
     and so doubling,
          and yet
buddings of the node
          upon a single cane, *cattleya*
with two
     opening
          on year's shortest day
and still blooming,
          three months later
in their paradigmatic
petals.

          Epiphytic, they think nothing of the absence
of God, that exogamic bee
          bargaining with wasps,
     or how they are confined
          to tree fern and coconut fiber
cupped on the sill of a kitchen window,
but open
     because they,
          within themselves, beyond
permissions
          ("women as plants are a threat
          because they fall outside or beyond")
only turn
toward
               outside...
                         beyond...

as
  we fall
turning
to

the luminous

petaling

of love glimpsed and becoming
                "a becoming-wasp of the orchid and a becoming-orchid
                of the wasp"

                Is there anything but
this turning
          so flowering
intricate
      labellum
          whether in the white and creamy yellow
                    in the underworld
                              "the part played by the subconscious"
or in gentle light and house,
                "what is the miracle of recognition?"
                or within
                    that mountain stream
tonguing
its way
      over rocks
              outside the window
                      "one thing changes into another, metamorphosis
          allows one to recognize
                    the other within"
running
            through me, or in a vision
when

the blue eyes of frozen saint
                    in dim niche
                            of church
became
        waves,
                infinite distances in a finite space, breaking
                        "virginity of mind is a sin"
into
        laughing presences.

                            All
so opening the corolla
to stamen
            here where the river of lost souls
                    and the other named for an ecstatic
conjoin in declensions of green
                a fruiting of orchards,
                            the blossoming peach
                                and savoring
later upon the tongue
            and lips
                    in rivulets of seasons—

                    "male by their testicular signature,
female by their seduction,
                    particularly ambiguous. In fact, their sex depends
on the observer…"

Ah, nothing so lovely
        as spring in the desert—
the air
            itself flowers

in sepals of blue
            and I would not have

felt this
            but for the sexual tongue
of a single bird
            of unidentified name

                        "by some secret law we recognize each other"
rippling
through my sleepwalking
                morning, calling
me to the nothing
that is
        there
            and isn't

        "involved… in the process of dissemination…
            appear only to disappear… present only as they metamorphose
                        themselves endlessly into other things"
waking that inaudible lilt
        rippling through the body,
                "a being at the same time indistinct and disturbing,"

so I find myself
awake suddenly
            at the threshold of the house,
laughing aloud
one moment

before opening the door
and going down
the steps into the interior

                singing
a ridiculous
        impromptu
out-of-tune tune

      "at once, femme fatale and Don Juan"
to the luminosities of orchids

just once
before everything darkens.

The empty hand

              is unmarried and not
engaged, is void of specified contents,
a knife for instance or a flaked stone,
and so is openly extended to, or held up
in calmest flower, above bloodstained
depths, beneath cerulean air. Vacant
and so unoccupied, gives itself to wind
and rain, is hungry and wanting fullness,
but is unburdened, has no carriage
to carry or horse to drive, bears no sweets
or furniture, brings and carries nothing
away, but leaves world as is, as it is
said of the biblical sword that to return
empty is to have slain no one. So many
senses, but without sense, it wants and
wants solidity and substance, a cup of soup
to warm its chill, the heavy shotglass of
intoxication, a silver dolphin curved around
the rim, entwined and riding in its fingers,
but, less open in grasp or fist, lets go and falls,
of any gift but itself, pours out, draws out,
draws upon the surface of the pond, palms
of hands, leaves of lilies, quietly riding upon
the body's river, clears the air and waves it
full of gestures. Flowers on those waters,
where anyone who loves is empty-handed;
all that loves, an open hand.

Don't Sing Me a Song of Conquest

sing me a song of the parrot,

for when María de Agreda, the lady in blue,
flew to New Mexico through the heavens

of the seventeenth century, while her body
lay, forsaken and drowsy, back

in a chapel in Spain, the thick-billed flock
must have flown beside her,

their profuse green clouds tapping a wilder rhythm
than the beat of her rosary, her cloth scapular

loosely noosed around her neck.
Don't sing me a song of the soul flying—

like a dandelion seed, triumphant, to disseminate
the word of God, a thorn traveling by foot,

transplanted from the City of God;
sing the lapsed song of

the cries of parrots,
earsplitting heaven

from a half mile away, their red shoulders
pressed to the lips of the sky.

Miraculous, the conquering fathers thought,
when the Indians they went to convert

parroted the sermons of the lady in blue,
captivity breaking their native tongue

to a stammering *kuk-kuk-kuk;*
by then, the remnants of those airy tribes fleeing

to Mexico to live in a few surviving forests
with their altricial young.

O lightning beneath those wings,
sing me a song of elsewhere, where you may still

live, though dying out for us: elsewhere
the beak of the parrot, still neatly hinged

with the mobility of a third foot,
in visitations, not exalted as seraphim

of imperial scion, but scaling a dusty piñon
with zygodactyl feet—

the two outer toes pointing backward
and the two inner toes pointing forward.

For here, before this cedar tree,
so many trunks rising out of a single root,

in that ancient aromatic foliage, I cannot even begin
to imagine the green gathering

of all the silences
we have created in this world.

In the Name of the Tyrant

What did we suffer for? why did we flee
our houses as if we had been hostages at our own
tables? Even free, we were not free, we kept
breaking down in thrift stores, our eyes
tearing in bins of glasses taken from the faces
of the dead; disoriented and dizzy as crows
swarming the corpses of our own hearts,
in the aisles of the department stores
filled with the glitter of plenty, we kept
spilling coffee on ourselves. Why
are we forever afraid of bathtubs, of water
hitting us in the face like the invisible
stoning of an anonymous crowd, why does buying
makeup make us feel guilty, why do we
eat our food like thieves? Why do we
sneak our friends in the back door
and make our love climb up a tree? Why
do our lies nest within one another like
diminishing dolls? Why do we jump
when the smallest child pushes open a door?
Why are we afraid of the whistling of teapots?
Who's coming in to read over our shoulders
our most secret thoughts, who's clinging
to our roofs like a demon? Why is his cheerfulness
even more frightening than his anger? Why does my hope
burn like the scar of a burn on my breast? Why are you
an eye floating in a pool of dead water, blue, and unable
to breathe? Why do we keep asking why?
How do we know how to stop it if we don't know
why it began? How can we unravel so much
violence followed by so much lie? How will we know
when it's ever over? or believe
it will ever stop?

In that language, "we two" is a first person dual pronoun

as in: "I" have a bag full of jokes, a dragonfly's
eye with which any
perception can be faceted into
a thousand equilateral views: "You"

could say it is the eye of equanimity,
though someone else might say
it is the eye of division.
In its gaze nothing is singular:

you will look through this eye
for the one (I) you love
and find a multiplicity,
a fracturing of the one into many, her face

reflected in so many pools of light,
that you will become convinced,
you are only a darkness.
You will be dragged

down into the pool
of sacrificial water
by the limitations
of your "self,"

for after all, for all you may admire
the gaze of the dragonfly,
you do not have its iridescent wings
that balance so precisely

at the edge of the water.

This is the page
you can look through,
though it resists

you by catching "you"
in a net of words.

Or perhaps it's this microscope you want,
that relic of childhood with its faith
in discovery and the power
of illumination, the instrument

so full of the difficulties
of illumination. Remember
the arduous process
by which you tried to catch

just enough light from the sun
in that tiny and cheap mirror?
As flawed as you are, it was still
needed to light up

everything, just as you have nothing
but your "self" as a hinge
for opening the door
to the world.

If you look into this depth,
you will find that self (whose?)
embodying the mystery of a remote
and weary god,

as you slip the slide with its raindrop
of light into the clips of the mount
and bring into focus these struggling
cells, their mouths a galaxy

of want and desire, their tails
flogging themselves forward,
the weaker ones flagging
at the edge of the drop,

"that pond," "that lake,"
you have created in order to view
what you cannot see by the naked eye,
the diminished and isolated
selves…

> *Look, all I want is to love you*
> *as we should love everyone…*

> "Even that boy
> with no shirt
> and the look of a well-oiled seal who
> is beating something senseless
> in the pudgy sunlight
> while his mother with the face of a desert
> and the hands of an eight-year-old girl reaching
> for *everything, everything, everything*
> haggles over a vacuum?"

"Be quiet, I can't think, there's the telescope,
rattling around, not quite fitting
in the bag, its long eye as distant
as you are, almost a miracle really

bringing you the constellations
of knowledge that infect you
with certain impossible
and vain desires,

like touching the wing
of that extinct parrot
on that most distant branch,
to touch the sadly nibbled fingers

of the beloved, chewed back
as they are by anxiety,
for whatever stars may light up
the limitations of the glass,

that darkness will remain
within her, a kind of space that calls to you
with the mysteriousness
of open feeling, but that you may

come to confuse
with the much nearer and more familiar
darkness that has always existed
in you."

                                            Well, as much
                                        as it hurts to walk
                                    around like one on fire,
                                            I'm afraid
                                            "I" am
                                                more
                                            of the ashes,
                                        that damp stench
                                    of what is extinguished
                                    permeating the house.

And, perhaps, that "love"
that you speak of is only
language. The field glasses,
for instance, full of the information

of war, you've forgotten how you plot
and eye the minefield that you are,
watching the thick woods on the other side
of the river, for the flash of bayonets, for every

relationship is a kind of war, in which you either fight
with the one you love or fight with yourself
on behalf of the other, which I've always thought,
personally speaking, is what Kafka meant

when he wrote, in "the fight between
yourself and the world, back the world,"

for he couldn't have been merely advocating
bowing to a superior force. He must have meant

the necessity of preferring the cause of the other
to the cause of oneself, as difficult as that may be.
Simone Weil would have said, "true friendship is rare"
and, truthful most of the time,

these field glasses will be uncanny with luck,
finding the right spot in the enemy line
where the young soldiers have fallen asleep,
or by chance, picking some number out of the air

to suggest that you don't want to be "passionate
friendship 105" thinking it is a mere number,
harmless as the dust cloud rising at random
along that distant road, not realizing

it is the very number
that has wounded your enemy (which is,
to say, the one you love), and the scar
of the arrow has not yet faded,

just as those dust risings along the road
are legions of warriors leaping onto their horses,
sent by the one you love (which is to say,
the one who is now your enemy),

riding toward you furiously, because
this morning, still drowsy with sleep, they caught
the glimmering flash of your field glasses
and knew they were under attack.

> "Yes, I remember
> the time I was sitting at the kitchen table
> and she came over and placed this knife
> in front of me and said 'here is the knife
> with which you will kill me.'

                                        I hardly knew what to say.
                              I was so shocked, I said something
                       ironic, my usual method of self-defense,
                something like, 'I wouldn't go to the trouble,'

                   and later when I said I was sorry for my ironic
                       remark, she said it was okay, that she knew
                              I was sorry by the catch in my breath,
                                     which must have been the sound
                                     of the other knife, the invisible one
                                                            of language,
                              which she had just driven into me."
             But what of the knife? The knife, oh
                       of course,
                       the knife;
                   it's still there upon the table.
Can't we throw this stuff out? Aren't you sick
of this junk? Your grandmother's dentures
still gnashing at your grandfather after fifty years
because he wanted to dance with that other 'girl,'
their neighbor's wife in her sixties? The clipping
that your father left in his thesaurus when the woman
he wanted to be his second wife married
someone else? The three faded leaves
of your first rejection, those strawberries
you could not find, so much junk you've picked up
from casual relationships and conversations, which you've kept
just in case you need them, digging through another's trash
for what might be useful,
so 'you' can see
as 'others' do, perceive what 'they' perceive? Just face it,
you're never going to understand how 'you' exist in the world,
how 'you' are perceived by others, how they believe
in those images of you that walk about in your clothes, wearing
your name, and yet whose semblances turn to you
with a gaze of fog, so 'you' become tumid

to your own eye/'I', as if being itself
were a kind of seasickness, as once,
standing in a bookstore full of strangers
waiting for a reading, I was talking
to my former lover's new lover and realized
that everyone in the room had her body
in common, and that I felt guilty about being
the first, for hadn't she said to me, tears
running down her cheeks, how everyone
was just "a pale reflection of you" as if being

in 'me' had sent her off to a life of replication
and recurrence in which what mattered
most was less the multiplication
of the flesh than the reproduction of the original sorrow.

                I think we are beginning to sound alike
                      in some dislocated cave
                          of wood
          where one makes a house out of the demarcations
                on the forest floor, of fallen branches,
                      the sweeping away
                    of the fallen pine needles,
                the other plays at 'home'
                    in the scraped earth.

Yes, I know, you've said this before,
you have difficulty thinking of yourself
at all, that's why, seeking some relief,
and I don't blame you for this,

you try to gaze through the petals
of the lily, a bit ridiculous, don't you think?
but it's still here, turning a bit brown
in the bottom of this bag, and yet

you think you can see through the flesh
of the world, as if through light itself,
the disembodied radiance that ignites
the pores with beauty, that hand

upon a table with its delineation
of muscles and veins, and you think
that this is a kind of spiritual love,
a sort of relief

to lay oneself down, dreaming
among the lilies, like a sheath
that has forgotten the sword,
bending your neck

to the hand or the blade
of the light that seems to fall
upon you like the inscrutability of God;
at this point, though, memory usually drags

you back into the inventory of the bag.
Though the quartz will suggest to you
the serenity of geological layers,
you'll kid yourself, you'll think

perhaps in another life, or on another
level of hell or paradise, for it's the level
that matters, not where,
you will find the other

and yourself
in some hierarchy of angels
or ranking of principalities
and will experience at least the certainty

with which the starfish
clings to the rock in the tidal pool, her arms

around your neck,
but I begin to think 'you'

do not exist, that I am really talking
to myself.

                                        And who is that?
                                        Blah, as common
                                                as any mirror,
                                        any shard will do
                                                to create
                                        the same weary
                                                resemblances.

Basically the secret name
of any mirror
is survival,
and that's why it's empty
until someone lends it a face.

                Where was I?
                                Who are you anyway?
                        What are 'you' but the hand that picked
                        up various sorrows and carried them here?
I know what 'I' am, I am a 'poet,' which is to say
a peddler of words, dragging
along all the dust and clatter of Babel,
and so many others—I meant to say *other things*

but it's others, too: a bag full of the roots
of what can never be transplanted,
a very small bag as heavy
as a collapsed star full of all

the secrets that I have been told,
another full of severed wings,

which can be heard at night
rustling trying to find

their way out,

which drives me to language
drives me to silence—
which drives me to silence,
as I am driven to you,

which is not much different from
my grandfather and his twin brother
peddling their bars of soap
in the Alpine valleys
until they strayed into another
country, for I am always straying
into another world.

I thought then if I stopped writing, I would die,
but not even death can stop the language, the dead
are yammering all the time, I don't need to see
what I'm trying to write, it's for others to read,
that's why there's no way to laugh on paper besides
writing *hahaha,* only the reader can laugh, I'm just
the darkness on the other side of the page.

Is that your brother dead in the field?
Or is that yourself?

God has given you one face,
you have made for yourself another.

O grant me the affectionate
touch of the tongue
and the soft smile of friendship.

Render useless the cruel
traps and snares.

Let me not be drunk
on what is poisonous.

                                        Set no dead corpse
                                                before me.

Let mercy and goodness
follow me all the days of my life.

                                        Let my heart not be caught
                                                in a cage of snow.

May the word that flies
out of...

                                                fly into...
                        as the syllable of that original tongue

                that you may not break,
                that I may not be broken.

Until the Cuticles Bleed

It's not the desire to wound but the desire
for perfection that makes one gnaw
upon oneself: that one good nail, spared the ruin
of the others. Some impossible idea
to smooth out any ragged edge that makes
a hand into a paw, a wounded thing of wince,
unable to pick up a needle or to thread an eye,
so wounded and so wounding, that the buttons
of that lovely dress that once fell so lightly away
are torn off in one's grip and clatter tactlessly to floor.

Love forced to be bodiless

dreams of a body,
                as a tree
in its red aromatic heartwood
dreams of leaves and roots,

               for the page
is the flesh of a tree, the page is
the *corpus luteum* of the lover,
                    the eye
falls upon the words as if
they were the "I" of the
               beloved,
a hand holds the page as if touching
the skin of the beloved,
               the words fall
through the body of the one reading
as blood falls and rises through
                 the body
of the one writing, the page is a wound
that bleeds words, the body is
                the wound
of the tree, the page is torn from the skin
of the lover, the page is
          torn
from the white birch, the lover wounds
the tree in order to write upon its skin
                  the love
of the beloved, upon the skin of the world
and the flesh of the tree with a tiny twig
                  a fragment
from the branches of the very same tree,
sharpened by the desire for
              the body of words

into a wounding thing, for the body
is dreaming of being bodiless
                              pouring over
the page like ink, like the black blood
of the wounded tree,
                    to be
is to be
a wound dreaming of speech, the page is
                                knotted
with the nots of being, the one writing
is full of the not of the self, and so is the one
                                    reading,
but they lie down in the yes of the page,
the yes that is torn from the tree, and there
                          (where else)
                              always dreaming itself
into existence, as if every word
were a lover, wounding itself into love's
                              worlding

CITY BOMBARDED WITH ICICLES

barrier tape is still bandaging trees
       its crime-scene garishness
torn away overnight by the living
       passing through, perimeters
  closed

for icicle warnings:

  those transparencies thickened

to stalactite honed

by a roof's slow drip

       to clumped ice dams above heads
       dangerous architecture
keeping pedestrians
on their toes, a crash the size of a car impending
above a threshold,
       some squared to drain pipes
reaching from roof to street,
       others as long as two or three floors
of menacing overhead
       and that burst of sun
melting
frozen fists to   a sigh of one slipping loose
strangest blow of heaven
       this time chunks harmlessly into the walk, strangest blow
of heaven, breaking the window
of a car,
       strange
as a window
       falling from its chain suspended
above the cafeteria's table

to shatter upon
the head of one child
		wearing a frame of brokenness around her neck,
		a jag sheering toward her throat,
how to move through this new terrain
		dangerous for people down here
dangerous for people up there
that man		whacking ice
from his roof
		the postal carrier
gauging the drip, drip, drip
		of threat, different
		risks of freezing
		falling
wings, not clouds or lazy circling eagles, but icicle-related injuries
		along the walkways,
so many
unnamed, unknown
		looking up in something like alarm,
		uncertain
where is the clear path for getting to school on Monday
		winding one's way through,
		so much new is unknown,
even those clumped bushes, each one a shock of wiry sprigs
knotted to one root
		whiplike, stripped of leaves,
nothing left but a host of tiny red berries
		what are they called? why always forgetting to ask?
the only color blooming
in ice so many
		could be galaxies constellated
to random, aperiodic order,
		arrayed in mythic figure and story ripening
before any eye has been born
with power to see and fix them to imagined
		shape, though the new stories perhaps

would resemble the old, the heart evolves so slowly
        and there are only a few predictable ends,
        are they edible? poisonous?
    and to whose tongue?

perhaps some creature
could eat them and go on singing,
        or are they some variety, human cultivars
cultivated to appeal
to the garden's predictable shapes of temptation unmeant
        for living hand or tongue
beautiful singularity,
        piercing intensities of red
and specificities
of shape, which resist metaphor while inviting

drops of blood?

        like those leeched carefully
from the acupuncturist's tiny lancet
        extracting
too much heat or too much masculinity or femininity
        from a particular body or draining
the anguish
        of pressure point?
or self-contained
        shining in their
spheres, like eggs or earths,
        each one a tiny world meant to seed some meadow
they will splinter and burst
        to reach, be willingly devoured,
consumed into another,
        or like the seed some saint envisions on the hand of god
and sees all world, all eye,
        dreaming within, or was that a fig or a nutmeg?
or perhaps secular and many, their shapes
of young women's or men's nipples

brushed to erectile
breath or hand,
        but, no, only the shape allows,
that color is rather
        of lips bit to blood, lipstick, something, nothing but what
        associating mind brings
as the fool wandering a field of snow brings along weeds of fled
        goathead in heel, burr in palm, festered nettle
beneath the skin
themselves, too bright, inutterable, unnamed, in this field of snow
        the transport,
transplantation, accidental transmigration, you
        who have no name for what you walk among
as the sun transpires in the skin of the berries
transects the hazarded edges,

    and that legion of frozen angels

begins to loose its grip
and falls
shattering or merely
melting into the melting earth

The Heart Might as Well Be a Freight Train

When I went back to the other car
to ask for aspirin for a child's
headache, she was flirting with some
young man of suave complexion
and glittering energy, and turned
to me with a kind of shock, a going
flat upon her face, a kind of guilt,
I thought later, so startling in its
atonality, that in asking for the aspirin,
I laughed abruptly to myself, for
what could I say to take back that guilt
upon her face, when I had gone
against the rhythm of the train
to ask only for aspirin for someone
else's pain. What collided in her
was like those cars coupled together,
a hand grasped around a wrist or a tongue
locked in a mouth, dragging along
the so many upon that train in one
inevitable direction. I was touched,
in a way, as if her guilt acknowledged
the existence of some grasp she held me
in, within herself, invisible clutch of her own
feeling that she felt only when she felt
it tightening—that gasp when she saw
me suddenly standing there, saying her name
to ask for aspirin. As if dragged back
to whoever she was with me, while she was being
someone else talking to someone else, both
of whom did not know me, and what could
I say then to release that grasp of self
upon the self? All so many thronging
within, that crowded train rocking down

downhill to its tawdry station,
dismayed by her dismay, I took
the aspirin back to my car and gave it
in ministrations to the child, then sat
feeling that secret marriage that jealousy
and guilt make, that hot flare in momentary
answer, oh vertigo to be so seized
in her gaze, all desire for possession
welling up in her look as if *possessed.*

How many fires

have I started
like this,
breathing into it

as if it were a drowned
child that I kept trying
to revive?
Caring nothing for my own
                                    hair, fingertips,
as I pressed closer
to the fire…
            yet the singeing of one hair, the sting
of one spark upon
the skin, and I leapt back
instinctively.

                        And because I am tired,
                  and want to stop thinking
of this fire of my fire for you, I kick the logs apart,

though my violence, which scatters them,
makes them burn the more.

                  Oh how can I leave you? except
to regret my own forcefulness;
                        in the morning, there will be nothing left
but a bed of ash,

            and a remnant or two, so carbonized with resentment,

will lie beneath
the grate of the campfire ring
and turn into an eye of smoke.
            O fire instruct me and make me wise,
for in you, I see how impossible

                              it is
               to make one log burn
                        alone,

though it might catch
          upon this conflagration
                    of tiny dead twigs
                                   I tore

from the dry limbs
of the ponderosa
pine—
          its amber blood
now the pitch
                    sparking
into flame—

but as quickly as the brambles of the wild
          that I gleaned from the meadow
                    of the soaring
                              transepts of silver
                                        and black butterflies
ignite
          in some winged and burning formlessness
          the obdurancies of red heartwood
                    its torn and lovely flesh
                                   smelling of aromatic
                    cedar, my love, my love,
falls upon itself
                              and smolders out.

          What did I think
                    when I was a child and on nights
                              like this, cold in the forest of myself,
                                        stared into
          the face of fire?

I was all longing
then,

all incipient flame, not full of the materiality of fate, that
            weighted thing, so full of rain and damp, gnawed by the tracks

of what has tried
to live within it,

            all those mouthed insistences making
a cave, a burrow, a kind of house
            out of living flesh.

Oh, who am I?
            And who are you?
(Who tried to burn her love letters and could not
contain the flames?)

It's not the proximity
            that makes these two pieces of cedar, their heads touching, begin
            to kindle, licked by a slower blue

that flares into orange and crimson
tongues,
            but the angle

of their inclination,
            the air itself between them
                    burns, the distances

ignite
their edges

            and make of us a fiery form, a flux and flow

a tactile intertwining: as if it were enough (it is never enough) that

            beauty is a consuming gaze.

NOTES

The opening quote is a mix, interweaving the commentary of Herbert Lockyer from *All the Parables of the Bible: A Study and Analysis of the More Than 250 Parables in Scripture* with the passages of James 3 in the King James Bible to which Lockyer refers, and I have also added the numbers.

"Take off your clothes…" by Robert Desnos, translated by the author.

"The wild is not destitute of flavor": The phrase "bleak and mountainous district" is from *The National Gazetteer of Great Britain and Ireland* (1868).

"Wild Tongue": The epigraph as well as the lines "Appearance does not really appear, but it appears to appear," "Does it really appear to appear, or only apparently appear to appear?" and "Whenever a number of individuals have a common name, they also have a common 'idea' or 'form'" are from Bertrand Russell's *The History of Western Philosophy*.

"Beyond Ithaca": "Poetry begins where death is robbed of the last word" is a quote from Odysseus Elytis.

"Night Music": I thought of this title and then later remembered that Muriel Rukeyser has a poem with the same title; though it was not meant to be reflective, perhaps it is. "He said that everything would change" is a reference to César Vallejo, who said that everything would change by using the word *radio*.

"The Avatar of Immanence": The "whale" of this poem is the orca, which is actually of the family *Delphinidae* (oceanic dolphins), but I have used the idiomatic "whale" and dubious "killer whale" to suggest the conversational commonality against which the woman retells her very different narrative.

"Editorial Advice": It was James Wright who said, with regard to reading literary journals and small magazines, that afterward he wanted to go out and lie facedown on the ground.

"Thieves of Fire": The title is taken from Rimbaud's phrase, "*Donc le poète vraiment voleur de feu.*"

"The erotic is the spark in the tinder of knowing" is a quote from Kenneth Rexroth.

"The Fragments of Hölderlin": I am indebted to Wilhelm Waiblinger's essay "Friedrich Hölderlin's Life: Poetry and Madness" (1830), translated by Scott J. Thompson, and also to some lines of Hölderlin's, though they were translated and retranslated through various online translation generators and much changed.

"Muse of Translation": The quotations are from *The Nemean Odes of Pindar* by John Baguell Bury (Pindaros) (1890). "There is no muse for philosophy and there is no muse for translation" is a paraphrase from Walter Benjamin.

"On the Island of Bones": "The poet looks at the world as a man looks at a woman" is a quote from Wallace Stevens. "With this prodigious ambition one begins" is from "What the Twilight Says: An Overture" by Derek Walcott.

"Fiction Weaving": The wordplay at the end of the poem plays upon a list of terms that have been used to refer to lesbians. *Chestnut gatherer, molly,* and *margery* were used in England in the nineteenth century and earlier; *perisexual,* though most commonly used to denote gay men in more scholarly writing, was also used to denote gay women (apparently following the omnibus theory); etc.

"*Unknowing*": The quotations are from *Herbarium Verbarium: The Discourse of Flowers* by Claudette Sartiliot (University of Nebraska Press, 1993).

CITY BOMBARDED WITH ICICLES was a headline in the *Boston Globe* in December 2005.

ABOUT THE AUTHOR

Rebecca Seiferle's poetry, translations, and essays have appeared in many journals and over twenty-five anthologies, and her poetry has been translated into several languages. She is the founding editor of the online international poetry journal *The Drunken Boat*, www.thedrunkenboat.com. Seiferle has a B.A. from the University of the State of New York with a major in English and history, and a minor in art history. In 1989, she received her M.F.A. from Warren Wilson College. She taught English and creative writing for a number of years at San Juan College and has taught at the Provincetown Fine Arts Center, Key West Literary Seminar, Port Townsend Writers' Conference, Gemini Ink, the Stonecoast M.F.A. program, and most recently was Jacob Ziskind poet-in-residence at Brandeis University. In 2004 she was awarded a poetry fellowship from the Lannan Foundation. She lives in Tucson, Arizona.

Copper Canyon Press gratefully acknowledges the
Lannan Foundation for supporting the publication and
distribution of exceptional literary works.

LANNAN LITERARY SELECTIONS 2007

Maram al-Massri, *A Red Cherry on a White-tiled Floor: Selected Poems*
Norman Dubie, *The Insomniac Liar of Topo*
Rebecca Seiferle, *Wild Tongue*
Christian Wiman, *Ambition and Survival: Becoming a Poet*
C.D.Wright, *One Big Self: An Investigation*

LANNAN LITERARY SELECTIONS 2000–2006

Marvin Bell, *Rampant*

Hayden Carruth, *Doctor Jazz*

Cyrus Cassells, *More Than Peace and Cypresses*

Madeline DeFrees, *Spectral Waves*

Norman Dubie, *The Mercy Seat: Collected & New Poems, 1967–2001*

Sascha Feinstein, *Misterioso*

James Galvin, *X: Poems*

Jim Harrison, *The Shape of the Journey: New and Collected Poems*

Hồ Xuân Hương, *Spring Essence: The Poetry of Hồ Xuân Hương,*
translated by John Balaban

June Jordan, *Directed by Desire: The Collected Poems of June Jordan*

Maxine Kumin, *Always Beginning: Essays on a Life in Poetry*

Ben Lerner, *The Lichtenberg Figures*

Antonio Machado, *Border of a Dream: Selected Poems,* translated by
Willis Barnstone

W.S. Merwin
The First Four Books of Poems
Migration: New and Selected Poems
Present Company

Taha Muhammad Ali, *So What: New & Selected Poems, 1971–2005,* translated by Peter Cole, Yahya Hijazi, and Gabriel Levin

Pablo Neruda
The Separate Rose, translated by William O'Daly
Still Another Day, translated by William O'Daly

Cesare Pavese, *Disaffections: Complete Poems 1930–1950,* translated by Geoffrey Brock

Antonio Porchia, *Voices,* translated by W.S. Merwin

Kenneth Rexroth, *The Complete Poems of Kenneth Rexroth*

Alberto Ríos
The Smallest Muscle in the Human Body
The Theater of Night

Theodore Roethke
On Poetry & Craft: Selected Prose of Theodore Roethke
Straw for the Fire: From the Notebooks of Theodore Roethke

Benjamin Alire Sáenz, *Dreaming the End of War*

Ann Stanford, *Holding Our Own: The Selected Poems of Ann Stanford*

Ruth Stone, *In the Next Galaxy*

Joseph Stroud, *Country of Light*

Rabindranath Tagore, *The Lover of God,* translated by Tony K. Stewart and Chase Twichell

Reversible Monuments: Contemporary Mexican Poetry, edited by Mónica de la Torre and Michael Wiegers

César Vallejo, *The Black Heralds,* translated by Rebecca Seiferle

Eleanor Rand Wilner, *The Girl with Bees in Her Hair*

C.D. Wright, *Steal Away: Selected and New Poems*

Matthew Zapruder, *The Pajamaist*

The Chinese character for poetry is made up of two parts: "word" and "temple." It also serves as pressmark for Copper Canyon Press.

Since 1972, Copper Canyon Press has fostered the work of emerging, established, and world-renowned poets for an expanding audience. The Press thrives with the generous patronage of readers, writers, booksellers, librarians, teachers, students, and funders—everyone who shares the belief that poetry is vital to language and living.

Major funding has been provided by:

Anonymous (2)

The Paul G. Allen Family Foundation

Beroz Ferrell & The Point, LLC

Lannan Foundation

National Endowment for the Arts

Cynthia Lovelace Sears and Frank Buxton

Washington State Arts Commission

For information and catalogs:

COPPER CANYON PRESS

Post Office Box 271

Port Townsend, Washington 98368

360-385-4925

www.coppercanyonpress.org

This book is set in Adobe Garamond and Sackers Gothic. Adobe Garamond, a digital interpretation of the roman types of Claude Garamond and the italic types of Robert Granjon, was designed by Robert Slimbach for Adobe, Inc., in 1989. Sackers Gothic was designed by the Linotype design studio. Book design and composition by Phil Kovacevich. Printed on archival-quality Glatfelter Author's Text at McNaughton & Gunn, Inc.